THE TRAGEDY OF MARIAM

THE TRAGEDY OF MARIAM
The Fair Queen of Jewry

Elizabeth Cary

edited by
Stephanie Hodgson-Wright

broadview literary texts

2503274   822·3
C AR

Canadian Cataloguing in Publication Data

Cary, Elizabeth, Lady, 1585 or 6-1639
    The tragedy of Mariam, the fair queen of jewry

(Broadview literary texts)
Includes bibliographical references.
ISBN 1-55111-043-1

1. Mariamne, consort of Herod I, King of Judea, ca. 57-ca. 28 B.C. – Drama.
2. Herod I, King of Judea, 73-4 B.C. – Drama. I. Hodgson-Wright, Stephanie.
II. Title. III. Series.
PR2499.F3T72 2000   822'.3   C00-930910-1

Broadview Press Ltd., is an independent, international publishing house, incorporated in 1985.

North America:
P.O. Box 1243, Peterborough, Ontario, Canada K9J 7H5
3576 California Road, Orchard Park, NY 14127
Tel: (705) 743-8990; Fax: (705) 743-8353
E-mail: customerservice@broadviewpress.com

United Kingdom:
Turpin Distribution Services Ltd.,
Blackhorse Rd, Letchworth, Hertfordshire SG6 1HN
Tel: (1462) 672555; Fax: (1462) 480947
E-mail: turpin@rsc.org

Australia:
St. Clair Press, P.O. Box 287, Rozelle, NSW 2039
Tel: (02) 818-1942; Fax: (02) 418-1923

www.broadviewpress.com

Broadview Press gratefully acknowledges the financial support of the Ministry of Canadian Heritage through the Book Publishing Industry Development Program.

Text design by Hungry Eye Design.

PRINTED IN CANADA

Contents

Acknowledgements

This edition was first published as part of the Renaissance Texts and Studies Series by Keele University Press in 1996. I should like to acknowledge the support, encouragement and assistance of the following individuals and organisations in the completion of the first and the current edition:

Anthony Bentley, Boyd M. Berry, Michael G. Brennan, Lucius Cary, 15th Viscount Falkland, Susan Cerasano, Jane Donawerth, Jo Evans, Inga-Stina Ewbank, Alison Findlay, Danielle Fuller, Isobel Grundy, M. Claude Lannette, David Lindley, Marie Loughlin, Maureen Meikle, Susan J. Owen, Liz Paget, Arthur Pritchard, Adele Seef, Keith Sewell, James Shaw, Revd. M.B. Tingle, Betty Travitsky, Gweno Williams, Barbara Wright, Marion Wynne-Davies, Alison Younger, Shari Zimmerman, Northern Renaissance Seminar, the Society for the Study of Early Modern Women, Tinderbox Theatre Co., the English Department and Research Committee at Trinity and All Saints University College, the English Division and Graduate Research School at the University of Sunderland, and the staff and reprographics departments of the numerous libraries listed herein.

Abbreviations

Ant. Flavius Josephus. *The most auncient historie of the Jewes: comprised in twenty books.* Trans. Thomas Lodge. London: 1602. STC 14809.

Geneva *The Geneva Bible.* Ed. Lloyd E. Berry. London: University of Wisconsin Press, 1969, rpt. 1981.

MS Lille Cary ? Biography of Lady Falkland, c. 1650, MS A.D.N.xx., Archives dèpartementales du Nord, Lille.

OED *The Oxford English Dictionary* (second edition). Prepared by J.A. Simpson and E.S.C. Weiner. Oxford: Clarendon Press, 1989.

STC *A Short-Title Catalogue of Books Printed in England, Scotland, & Ireland...1475-1640,* (second edition). Ed. W.A. Jackson, F.S. Ferguson and K.F. Pantzer. Volume 1 A-H (1986); Volume 2 I-Z (1976); Volume 3 (1991). London: The Bibliographical Society, 1986-91.

Elizabeth Cary, first Viscountess Falkland, painted by Paul Van Somer, 1621. By kind permission of W.W. Winter Ltd., Derby, UK.

Introduction

The Author

Elizabeth Cary, née Tanfield, was born in 1585, in Burford, Oxfordshire. She was the sole child of the lawyer Laurence Tanfield and his wife, Elizabeth, and was known to be a precocious and learned child. The poet Michael Drayton, who may have been her tutor,[1] wrote in *Englands Heroicall Epistles* (1597):

> Sweete is the French tongue, more sweete the Italian, but most sweete are they both if spoken by your admired selfe. If Poesie were prayselesse, your vertues alone were a subject sufficient to make it esteemed though amongst the barbarous Getes:by how much the more your tender yeres give scarcely warrant for your more then womanlike wisedom, by so much is your judgement, and reading, the more to be wondred at. (Drayton G 3^V).

Clearly, Elizabeth had demonstrated her fluency in foreign languages well before she embarked upon her first surviving work, a manuscript translation of Abraham Ortelius' *Le Miroir du Monde* (Amsterdam, 1598).

At the age of seventeen, in 1602, she was married to Sir Henry Cary, son of Sir Edward and Lady Katherine Cary. The marriage, as was usual amongst families of the gentry and aristocracy, was arranged as a matter of social, political and economic expediency. Elizabeth Cary's daughter, in a biography written c. 1650,[2] tells us that "he maried her only for being an heir, for he had no acquaintance with her (she scarce ever having spoken to him) and she was nothing handsome, though then very faire." (MS Lille fol. 3^V) The significance of the financial arrangements of this marriage is also evidenced by John Chamberlain's letter of 27 June 1602, to Dudley Carleton:

Here is talke of a match . . . twixt Sir Henry Cary and Master Tanfeilds daughter with 2000^{li} presently, 2000^{li} at two yeares, and 3000^{li} at his death, yf he chaunce to have more children, otherwise to be his heir *ex asse*. (McClure 153)

The match was made in or by October 1602. However, apart from a Christmas spent with Sir John Harrington in Rutlandshire, together with "the earles of Rutland and Bedford, Sir John Gray . . . with theyre Ladies, the earle of Pembroke, Sir Robert Sidney and many moe gallants" (McClure 179), it is likely Henry and Elizabeth spent most of the first six years of their marriage apart. Their first child was not born until 1609 and the rapidity with which the children arrived after that date would seem to confirm that the couple did not share a bed on a regular basis for the early years of their marriage. Henry went to London in 1603 to pursue his career at the Court, then travelled to the Continent in 1604 and did not return until July 1606. Meanwhile, Elizabeth spent some time with her own family, but eventually gave in to pressure from her mother-in-law and went to live at the Cary family home. On Henry's return, Elizabeth took up the role of wife to an ambitious young courtier. While he rose through the ranks at court, eventually becoming first Viscount Falkland in 1620, she bore and nursed his children. The Falklands were uprooted in 1622, when Henry was appointed Lord Deputy of Ireland. During her stay in Ireland, Elizabeth realised that her growing affinity for the Catholic faith was too strong to be borne in silence. She threw herself into community projects in Ireland, but the sight of her husband persecuting Catholics with great relish became too much for Elizabeth and she returned to England in 1625.

In 1626 she converted publicly to Catholicism, to the annoyance of Charles I and the absolute outrage of her husband, who refused to give her any financial support. Elizabeth petitioned the King on several occasions, writing vigorously of her great want, but, despite gaining the express support of the King and the Privy Council, she never received maintenance from her husband. During this difficult time, Elizabeth gained the favour of some of the most influential women at court, including Katherine, Duchess of Buckingham, Susan, Countess of Denbigh, and Mary, Countess of Buckingham (the wife, sister and mother of the King's favourite). At one point, much to Henry's chagrin, Katherine interceded in the marital dispute on Elizabeth's behalf. Elizabeth's Catholicism and her fluency in French may have brought her close to Queen Henrietta Maria, to whom she dedicated, in the warmest terms, her translation of *The Reply of the Most Illustrious Cardinall of Perron* (Douay, 1630, STC 6385).

The stalemate between Elizabeth and her husband continued for five years, until Henry's death in September 1633 as a result of injuries sustained whilst shooting with the King in Theobalds Park. The next phase of Elizabeth Cary's life was to cause the King and his government even more concern than her estrangement from her husband. Confirmed in her Catholic faith, Elizabeth determined that her younger children should also become Catholics. Her four daughters, Lucy, Mary, Elizabeth and Anne, lived with her and were thus easily influenced, much to the concern of Archbishop Laud, who wrote to King Charles I to request him to reiterate his command "that she should forbear working upon her daughter's consciences and suffer them to go to my Lord their brother [i.e., Lucius Cary, second Viscount Falkland], or any other safe place where they might receive such instruction as was fit for them." (Simpson 178-79) Archbishop Laud was unsuccessful in his attempt to shield Elizabeth Cary's daughters from Catholicism. They became nuns at the Benedictine Convent of Cambrai between 1638 and 1639.

Archbishop Laud was similarly unsuccessful in his attempt to prevent the reception of Elizabeth Cary's two sons, Patrick and Henry, into the Catholic faith. With the help of her daughters, Elizabeth removed her sons from the household of their brother, Lucius, and sent them to France. Whilst there had been concern over the spiritual condition of Elizabeth Cary's daughters, the prospect of her sons converting to the Catholic faith brought the full force of the law down upon her. On 16 May 1636, Lord Chief Justice Bramston was called upon to examine Elizabeth and her accomplices, Harry Auxley and George Spurrier. The two men confessed everything, but Elizabeth gave evasive and ambiguous answers. As a result, she was called before Star Chamber on 25 May 1636 and was threatened with imprisonment in the Tower if she continued to be unhelpful. This threat did not work, nor does it appear to have been carried out. Both of Elizabeth's sons travelled to the Continent and were received into holy orders before their mother's death in October 1639. Little is known of the circumstances of Elizabeth's death, although her daughter's biography tells us that she was given a Catholic burial in Henrietta Maria's chapel at Somerset House.

Date of the Play

The Tragedy of Mariam must have been composed after 1603 and before 1612. The Dedicatory Poem tells us that Elizabeth Cary's first play was dedicated to her husband and that her second, The Tragedy of Mariam, was dedicated to her sister-in-law. As Elizabeth was not married until late 1602, it is unlikely she could have written either play before 1603. In 1612 Sir John Davies made her the joint dedicatee of The Muses Sacrifice, together with Lucy, Countess of Bedford, and Mary, dowager Countess of Pembroke. His dedication encouraged all the women to publish their work, and is possibly the reason why The Tragedy of Mariam eventually reached the printing press. Stanzas seventeen and eighteen of "The Epistle Dedicatory" praise Cary thus:

> Cary (of whom Minerva stands in feare,
>   lest she, from her, should get Arts Regencie)
> Of Art so moves the great-all-moving Spheare,
>   that ev'ry Orbe of Science moves thereby.
> Thou makst Melpomen proud, and my Heart great
>   of such a Pupill, who, in Buskin fine,
> With Feete of State, dost make thy Muse to mete
>   the Scenes of Syracuse and Palestine. (Davies * ∗ * 3ᵛ)

"Palestine" refers to *The Tragedy of Mariam* and "Syracuse" to Cary's first play.

When the evidence provided by the Dedicatory Poem is set against other documentary evidence, the range of possible composition dates narrows. The Dedicatory Poem refers specifically to Henry Cary's absence and the metaphor suggests removal to a foreign country. Henry left for the Continent in 1604 and returned in July 1606. Elizabeth was pregnant by early 1608 and the couple were not parted again for any significant length of time until many years later. The possiblity that Elizabeth Cary wrote her first play during the early months of her marriage and presented it to her husband before his departure is rendered unlikely by this extract from the biography:

> [Henry] in the time they had bene married, had bene for the most part att the court or his fathers house, from her, and had heard her speake little, and those letters he had receaved from her had bene inditted by others, by her mothers appointment. (MS Lille fol. 3ᵛ)

It is possible, then, that Elizabeth spent the early part of Henry's absence composing her first play. According to her daughter's biography, all of Elizabeth's books were taken away, by order of Lady Katherine Cary. The result was that "she sett herself to make verses" (MS Lille fol. 4ʳ). This must have been in 1604, as Elizabeth spent the first year of Henry's absence with her parents. Whether she embarked upon *The Tragedy of Mariam* immediately after finishing this first play, but before Henry's return, is debatable. The biography, in relating Henry's reaction to his wife on his return, says:

> In his absence he had receaved some letters from her, since she came from her mother, which seemed to him to be in a very different stile from the former, which he had thought to have bene her own;these he liked much, but beleeved some other did them; till having examined her about it, and found

the contrayry, he grewe better acquainted with her, and esteemed her more. From this time she writ many thinges for her private recreation, on severall subiects, and occasions, all in verse (out of which she scarce ever writ any thinge that was not translations) one of them was after stolen out of that sister inlaws (her friends) chamber, and printed, but by her own procurement was calld in. (MS Lille fol. 4ᵛ)

The suggestion that Henry encouraged her to write perhaps indicates that Elizabeth waited for her husband's approval before attempting a second play. If this is the case, then *The Tragedy of Mariam* might be dated no earlier than 1606.

Sources

The Tragedy of Mariam is based upon the story of Herod and Mariam as told by the Jewish historian Flavius Josephus in *The Antiquities* and *The Wars of the Jews*. These works first appeared in English in *The Famous and Most Memorable works of Josephus*, translated by Thomas Lodge in 1602. Although there were numerous European translations of Josephus available on the Continent, it is likely that Cary relied upon the Lodge translation, as there are various verbal similarities between the texts.

In his introduction to his edition of the play (xiv-xv), A.C. Dunstan points out the similarity between phrases in *The Tragedy of Mariam* and phrases in Lodge's translation. For example, in Cary's "The Argument" she says, "and presently after by the instigation of Salome, [Mariam] was beheaded" (38), which corresponds with Lodge's translation – "Marriame by Salomes instigation is led to execution" (*Ant.* 398). Likewise, when referring to the assassination of Aristobolus, Cary's Argument talks of how he was drowned "under colour of sport" (11), whereas Lodge has "pretending to duck him in sport" (*Ant.* 386). Finally, Dunstan refers to the line, "Am I the Mariam that presumed so much" (IV. viii. 1), which he says ties in with the Lodge translation thus: "For she being entertained by him, who entirely loved her . . . she presumed upon a great and intemperate libertie in her discourse" (*Ant.* 399).

In addition to those noted by Dunstan, there are several other instances of such verbal agreement. The phrase "under the colour of" or "under colour of" occurs more than once in Lodge's translation, most notably:

> under the colour of a high and magnanimous spirit, he made show to pardon [Alexandra] of his mere clemency: yet inwardly resolved he to make young Aristobolus away. (*Ant.* 385)

The idea of Mariam "presuming" also makes another significant appearance: "she presumed too much upon the entire affection wherewith her husband was entangled" (*Ant.* 398). Textual similarities are present in the Argument: "[Mariam] still bore the death of her friends exceeding hardly" (22), compared to Lodge's "she digested the loss of her friends also very hardly" (*Ant.* 399); "Unbridled speech is Mariam's worst disgrace" (III. iii. 65) compared to Lodge's "the too unbridled manners of [Herod's] wife" (*Ant.* 399); "I know that moved by importunity, / You made him priest" (IV. iii. 50-51) compared to Lodge's "Mariamme did continually importune him to give the priesthood to her brother" (*Ant.* 384). Moreover, Lodge has a character called "the butler," translated from the Latin "pincernam," and Cary has "Bu.", presumably a butler, as he brings Herod the cup of wine in IV. iii. Cary's use of the translation "butler" is particularly telling in comparison to other dramatic versions of the story. Alexandre Hardy in his play *Mariamne* (1605?) uses a term approximating to the English "Cup-bearer" rather than butler, presumably the result of using a French or Latin version of Josephus. Gervase Markham and William Sampson in *The True Tragedy of Herod and Antipater* (1622) conflate the character of the Cup-bearer with that of Pheroras, referring in the dramatis personae to "Pheroras, brother to Herod, and Cup-bearer" (Ross 6).

The source stories taken from *The Antiquities* and *The Wars of the Jews* take place over approximately twenty-eight years, from the marriage of Herod and Mariam in 35 BC, to the relationship between Salome and Silleus in 7 BC. Cary employs the classical unities of time, place and action to condense and re-work the stories into a play in which gender politics are set in sharp relief against a background of dynastic conflict and Roman imperialism. The unity of time is observed: the Chorus refers to the action as having taken place in "twice six hours" (Ch. V. 6). This allows for characters which bear no relation to each other in the source material to be juxtaposed as agents of the same dramatic theme, e.g., Salome and Doris (divorce); Silleus and Constabarus (chivalry and misogyny); Mariam and Graphina (chastity and humility). The entire action of the play is set in Judea, thus observing the unity of place. The unity of action is observed as the whole plot turns upon the belief in and subsequent discrediting of the rumour of Herod's death. The focus upon gender politics is further enhanced by the fact that the play keeps to the classical convention of a maximum of three speaking characters in any one scene. This prevents the presentation of any of the events in a public arena. For example, in the play Herod's decision to execute Mariam results from Salome working upon his paranoid anxieties, yet according to Josephus, Herod reaches his decision after Mariam has undergone a formal trial (*Ant.* 398).

Cary's main debt to Josephus lies in the plot-lines, which she adapts freely from her source. The bitter dynastic rivalry between Mariam and Salome is retained, as is Salome's use of the Butler to deliver the "poison" drink. Alexandra's explicit hatred towards Herod, followed by her duplicitous berating of Mariam on the way to her execution also features in the play, though the latter event is reported by the Nuntio in Act V. The Herod of the play, like the Herod of the source material, is a jealous obsessive tyrant, given to summary executions – i.e., Sohemus, Constabarus and Baba's sons – and whose moods are manipulated by his sister Salome. The false rumour of Herod's death is transposed from his first absence from Judea (summoned by Antony) to his second absence (summoned by Caesar). Cary lifts various events from her source and then makes a causal link between them and this false rumour. Instances of self-assertion, which Josephus relates as occuring independently of Herod's absence, owe their existence in Cary's play to this very absence, and are threatened by his return. Pheroras' marriage to his maid (the name Graphina is Cary's invention)[3] and Salome's divorce from Constabarus are both related by Josephus, but it is Cary who makes these two events a direct result of Herod's supposed death. The events are linked further, as each sibling agrees to speak in defence of the other on Herod's return. Similarly, according to Josephus, Constabarus hid Baba's sons and was eventually betrayed by Salome, but their brief liberation is Cary's invention.

Cary also makes several changes to the characters. Mariam is presented much more sympathetically by Cary than by Josephus. His Mariamme (sic) is prepared to be guileful towards her husband and is similarly active in winning the confidence of Sohemus, behaviour which is explicitly eschewed by Cary's Mariam. Cary draws Sohemus as a compassionate and devoted servant, whereas Josephus' Sohemus is calculating and self-interested. Cary makes a similar change in her depiction of Constabarus, whose protection of Baba's sons was, according to Josephus, a political hedge rather than an act of charity. Salome, whilst retaining her slanderous tongue and her hatred of Mariam, is given an entirely new characteristic by Cary: a penchant for changing husbands at will. Josephus shows no causal link between the death of Salome's first husband and her marriage to Constabarus. Furthermore, the play's vital link between Salome's divorce from Constabarus and his subsequent death in 28 BC and her relationship with Silleus in 7 BC is clearly a dramatic fiction, as is the sword fight between the two men. Cary also gives prominence to characters who receive only a brief mention by Josephus. Doris' return to Judea and her encounter with Mariam are completely original to Cary. The relationship between Constabarus and Baba's sons is greatly developed from a few sentences, and the sentiments expressed by them come from Cary's pen, not Josephus'. The Butler's suicide and Herod's reaction to it are also only to be found in the play.

Finally, Cary's decision to set the play entirely in Judea facilitates a radical change in focus from that of her sources. Josephus writes mainly of Herod and his political activities at home and abroad; Herod's household is merely an operational base. When Josephus relates Herod's return to Judea, it is described from his perspective, i.e., what Herod finds waiting for him at home. Cary's play takes exactly the opposite perspective, depicting Judea without Herod. The first three acts of the play are particularly significant in this respect, as they set prime importance upon the relationships between the women and upon the new found freedom which everyone (but particularly the women) have found now that Herod is believed to be dead. The striking "triumgynate" which dominates the majority of the first act could only have been brought about by major changes in the physical locations of the women. *The Antiquities* specifically states that Mariam and Alexandra were housed in the castle of Alexandria, whereas Salome was housed in the castle of Masada (*Ant.* 395) precisely to prevent the kind of dispute shown in I. iii. In Cary's version, then, the women are re-placed at the centre of power and imbued with freedom of speech and self-determination. Her employment of the classical unities foregrounds Judea, and particularly Herod's household, to which Herod becomes the destructive and intrusive "other."

Plot and Character

The plot of *The Tragedy of Mariam* turns on a simple "before and after" effect. Herod is believed to be dead, and as a result his family and servants choose courses of action that would have been impossible if he were alive. Herod unexpectedly returns, and his family and servants face the consequences of their behaviour. In the first part of the play, the characters explore the potential benefits resulting from Herod's absence. Whilst there are some sources of conflict among Alexandra, Mariam and Salome, this hardly constitutes, as Sandra K. Fischer claims, a failure "to offer a 'counter-universe' to the male oriented and dominated order" (Fischer 233). The factional squabbling results from the suspension of patriarchal rule, yet the freedom that all the characters enjoy is achieved precisely because of the absence of such rule. The nature of the interim government is ill-defined. Alexandra's words suggest that the political situation is still to be addressed:

> Let us retire us, that we may resolve
> How now to deal in this reversèd state:
> Great are th'affairs that we must now revolve,
> And great affairs must not be taken late. (I. ii. 125-28)

Herod's successor to the throne is still a boy, as Mariam indicates:

> My Alexander, if he live, shall sit
> In the majestic seat of Solomon. (I. ii. 62-63)

The characters refer to the new-found freedom in terms of Herod's absence, rather than the presence of a better and more benevolent government. Salome says, "My will shall be to me instead of law" (I. vi. 80), and Pheroras talks of Herod's absence as having "made my subject self my own again" (II. i. 8). Constabarus is free to liberate his friends from hiding now that Herod cannot harm them; Pheroras and Graphina are free to marry because Herod is not there to impose his will upon Pheroras' marital destiny, and Mariam is freed from the obligation of sleeping in Herod's bed. Most significantly, Salome, after the apparently irresolvable conflict with Alexandra and Mariam in I. iii, turns her mind to that which is possible – her relationship with Silleus. If her desire to marry him is fulfilled, then she will leave Jerusalem and live in Arabia, thus removing herself from the site of conflict. Salome's proposal to remove Constabarus is certainly less destructive than her method of removing her previous husband: divorce takes the place of execution. Doris' violent curses prove ineffective as does Silleus' attempt to duel with Constabarus. Once Herod returns and re-imposes his absolute authority, the consequences follow with the maximum violence and destruction. Six characters lose their lives as a result of Herod's return. Salome's plotting and dissembling are successful; Mariam's reliance upon her integrity contributes to her demise; Doris' desire for revenge upon Mariam is vindicated, and Herod himself suffers psychological torture as a result of his actions. As a counter-universe, the society of Acts I and II is not a failure; rather, it is presented as preferable to that which exists once the patriarch is re-established.[4]

In creating this contrast between Judean society with and without Herod in command, the play facilitates a debate about women's voices and women's bodies. The contemporary equation between an outspoken woman and an unchaste one is continually confounded. In the first part of the play, both Mariam and Salome are outspoken, but only Salome is presented as unchaste. In the second part of the play, Salome changes her vocal tactics in accordance with the return of Herod and thereby survives, whereas the still outspoken but chaste Mariam is executed as an adulteress. The two characters are clearly set in contrast to one another: Mariam is chaste and values highly her chaste reputation; Salome is unchaste and holds reputation in contempt. Mariam prizes her integrity; Salome excels in her ability to dissemble. They are cast as rivals, with the vengeful Salome being active in bringing about Mariam's death. However, critics have been too eager to read the difference in their characters as simple opposition, with Mariam as heroine and Salome as villainess.[5] This reading of the two characters obscures the extent to which they share one crucial quality – a desire for power over their own bodies – and the fact that they both seize the opportunity provided by Herod's absence to pursue that desire. Both Mariam and Salome distance themselves from the form of empowerment which is represented by Alexandra, Doris, and the frequently mentioned Cleopatra. All of these women seek to gain power and status by their relationships with males, regardless of whether or not those relationships are personally fulfilling.

For example, Doris is motivated by ambition for her son: if Herod will give Antipater the recognition he deserves, Doris asks nothing for herself. Mariam, however, gives primary consideration to the injuries done to herself and her family, and will not heed Sohemus' warning: "Yet for your issue's sake more temp'rate be" (III. iii. 31). Mariam also eschews the use of her body as a source of political empowerment:

Not to be Empress of aspiring Rome,
Would Mariam like to Cleopatra live:
With purest body will I press my tomb,
And wish no favours Antony could give. (I. ii. 121-24)

As well as making a moral judgement on Cleopatra, Mariam is rejecting the values of Alexandra's generation – the abdication of bodily power for the sake of political and economic gain. The cost of being Empress of Rome would be too high, if it meant another round of sexual subjugation. Sexual relationships, marital or otherwise, for the sake of political gain are, in Mariam's eyes, tantamount to licentiousness. In her final speech she characterizes Cleopatra as

The wanton Queen, that never loved for love
False Cleopatra, wholly set on gain. (IV. viii. 13-14)

For Mariam, submitting to the sexual advances of any man, husband or not, for motives other than love, is a form of unchastity. Therefore, she will not use her sexual allure to manipulate Herod:

I know I could enchain him with a smile
And lead him captive with a gentle word.
I scorn my look should ever man beguile,
Or other speech, than meaning to afford. (III. iii. 45-48)

In refusing to enter Herod's bed, Mariam tries in vain to hold on to the position in which she found herself at the beginning of the play. As a married woman refusing to enter into sexual relations with any man, including her husband, Mariam creates an anomalous position for herself. This is where her vulnerability lies, for Herod is unable to comprehend this anomaly, and reworks it in the only way available to him: if Mariam is refusing him access to her body, she must be allowing another man access in his place. As Luce Irigaray points out: "For woman is traditionally use-value for man, exchange-value among men. . . . Woman is never anything more than the scene of more or less rival exchange between two men." (Irigaray 105) The patriarchal ideology of the early seventeenth century did not allow for the concept of a female subject being in control of her own sexuality. Herod reworks the phenomenon of Mariam's rejection of him by constructing Sohemus as a successful rival for possession of her body in order to make sense of a situation incomprehensible to him. While her methods are very different, Salome also refuses to be such "use-value." She enters the marriage market on her terms, appropriating the conditions of Herod's regime to her own use. Therefore, once she prefers Constabarus to Josephus, she seizes the opportunity to betray Josephus to Herod, making her new marriage appear to be a by-product of her political orthodoxy. Herod's absence offers her the more radical opportunity to break with convention and wrest the law to her own use; in doing so she represents the full danger of a woman who has lost her reputation. With that gone, she is capable of anything because she has nothing left to lose:

> But shame is gone and honour wiped away,
> And impudency on my forehead sits.
> She bids me work my will without delay,
> And for my will I will employ my wits. (I. iv. 33-36)

Once Herod returns she reverts to her tried and tested methods, and arranges for Pheroras to betray Constabarus, making the divorce appear to stem from Salome's loyalty to Herod. Like Mariam, Salome eschews the use of her body for political gain. She has no interest in the riches and power which Silleus can offer her, and in fact states that he is the only reason she would contemplate leaving:

> Were not Silleus he with whom I go
> I would not change my Palestine for Rome. (I. v. 37-38)

Mariam chooses abstinence, Salome chooses indulgence, but both attempt to carve out positions for themselves outside of the economy of dynastic marriage.

Some critics, rather than simply seeing Salome and Mariam as diametric opposites, see Graphina and Salome as representatives of

the virtuous and vicious aspects of Maria⌐
lematic when one considers Graphina's s
This does not mean she is simply sociall⸝
it means that, by law, she does not ha⸝
Therefore, by marrying Pheroras, s⸝
economically dependent upon Pheroras, b⸜
dependent already. Nor does she stand to lose an⸝
tion because she never had any. It was because of his lo⸜
that Pheroras refrained from asserting his rights over her body:

> You have preserved me pure at my request,
> Though you so weak a vassal might constrain
> To yield to your high will. (II. i. 61-63)

By becoming Pheroras' wife, Graphina merely undergoes a process of *consenting* to the relationship based on the assumption of male sexual power under which she already lived (without giving her consent) as his slave. Thus, Pheroras and Graphina's relationship in II. i shows that the only means by which marriage can be played out in a mutually successful fashion is in the format of male master and female slave. Graphina's virtue cannot therefore be seen as an aspect of Mariam's, for Graphina's is a virtue born of socio-economic necessity.

Upon Herod's return, Salome turns her mind away from her radical wresting of Mosaic law and towards revenge against Mariam. Indeed, Herod's return is crucial in unleashing destructive female forces. Salome needs Herod to work her revenge; without privileged access to her brother's ear, and hence his absolute power, Salome would herself be powerless against Mariam. Similarly, the defeated Doris of Act II re-appears vindicated and triumphant in Act IV, to force the condemned Mariam to acknowledge that "Thy curse is cause that guiltless Mariam dies" (IV. viii. 84). Out of considerations of political expediency, Alexandra turns against her own daughter. And, ironically, Mariam sees her own integrity as ultimately a force of destruction:

d not myself against myself conspired,
No plot, no adversary from without,
Could Herod's love from Mariam have retired. (IV. viii. 9-11)

Whilst Mariam might be unaware of Salome's involvement in her demise, her own antagonism towards Herod is the root cause of her fate. Finally, in addition to the destruction heaped upon others, Herod's tyranny exhibits the seeds of its own destruction. Herod is also a victim of patriarchal ideology, for he suffers from the false consciousness of the ruling class; he believes he is in full control. Yet in order to retain his position, Herod must uphold the laws which validate that position. The ideologically imposed magnitude of female sexual transgression is so great that Herod is required to order the death of the woman without whom, as becomes apparent in V, his life is untenable.

She was my graceful moi'ty, me accursed,
To slay my better half and save my worst. (V. i. 133-34)

Taken literally, one half of the body cannot live without the other, and Herod ends the play expressing a desire to die.

Herod does not have the final word, however. That task falls to the Chorus, who speak at the end of each act.[7] Chorus I and II condemn the vices of discontent and gullibility respectively. The highly problematic nature of Chorus III has been most discussed in recent criticism. It apparently propounds the strictest rules for wifely behaviour, recommending that women do not even take the limited liberties allowed to them, yet is written by a woman venturing into the exclusively masculine discourse of original drama. Furthermore, its lines are broken into qualifying clauses, as if a subversive voice is trying to break through. The "one" of line 24 can be variously interpreted – husband, God, or, most radically, the wife herself. This is in fact the most logical interpretation; if a thought is to be known only to one person, that person must be the originator of that thought. The Chorus thereby suggests a withholding of self from the husband which is as radical as

Mariam's refusal to return to Herod's bed, for it casts the wife's mind as her best part. The final line perhaps best articulates the contradictions at the heart of this Chorus:

> Now Mariam had, but that to this she bent
> Been free from fear, as well as innocent. (Ch. III. 35-36)

The audience is reminded that Mariam dies innocent of any crime and that she is condemned merely because her outward demeanour is subject to the defining gaze of her husband and King. With this in mind, perhaps the first stanza is not didactic, but a statement delineating the outrageous imposition placed upon wives. Chorus IV condemns the desire for revenge, and recommends forgiveness as the preferable course of action. The final stanza focuses on Mariam, and tries, but ultimately fails, to suggest an appropriate course of action for her. The "virtuous pride" (Ch. IV. 35) of which it speaks is actually surrender and humiliation; this is how Mariam should have "been proud" in order to secure "long famous life" (Ch. IV. 35-36). Chorus V turns away from its role as moral commentator and sums up the main events of the play. Whilst directing the audience to see an educative message in these events, it also leaves the audience to decide the precise nature of that message.

Performance

Virtually all twentieth-century critics assign *The Tragedy of Mariam* to the genre of closet drama, despite the fact that the term itself is far from being well-defined.[8] This generic categorisation has resulted from Cary's likely links with Mary Herbert, Countess of Pembroke, and her literary circle at Wilton, possibly through her acquaintance with Michael Drayton and John Davies (see pp. 11, 14). Margaret Ferguson claims that "Cary's play is clearly indebted to that aristocratic experiment in Senecan closet drama" (Ferguson 235), and Barbara Lewalski says "In addition to this influential precedent by an aristocratic woman [i.e., *Antonie*], the closest analogues for

Mariam are other tragedies written by members of the Countess's circle: Samuel Daniel's *Cleopatra* and *Philotas*, and Fulke Greville's *Mustapha*." (Lewalski 191). There are certainly some similarities between *The Tragedy of Mariam* and the others, such as an Argument, a five-act structure and a Chorus, and it is also possible that Elizabeth Cary took her unusual quatrain rhyme scheme from Samuel Daniel's *Cleopatra* (London, 1594). Furthermore, many of the Wilton plays deal with events occurring during the early history of the Roman empire, which forms the political background to the events in Cary's play. However, the precise extent of Cary's debt to these dramas, and in particular to the Countess of Pembroke's own translation of Robert Garnier's *Antonie* (London, 1592), is still a matter for critical debate.[9] Diane Purkiss suggests Cary imitates Pembroke for socio-political reasons:

> Lady Pembroke, praised as the exemplary Protestant noble-woman and wife by her own coterie, and translator of Robert Garnier's trendsetting Senecan drama *The Tragedie of Antonie* [was] a possible role-model of female self-fashioning for a bookish young wife. . . . On marrying into the upper classes, Elizabeth Cary sets out her stall as a noblewoman by writing two Senecan dramas of her own, dramas which display the education she brings to her new circumstances and her appropriateness for them. (Purkiss xvi)

Yet, even if the Countess of Pembroke were a role model for Cary, Margaret P. Hannay's description of *Antonie* hardly applies to *The Tragedy of Mariam*:

> *Marc Antoine* is a drama of character, not of action; Garnier was not interested in events themselves, but in the refraction of events through different viewpoints, giving the perspectives of both the noble protagonists and their subjects. (Hannay 120)

In *The Tragedy of Mariam*, only the executions occur offstage. All other action is performed onstage, including the sword fight between

Constabarus and Silleus and the presentation of the "poison" cup to Herod. Indeed, the plot turns upon one major action: the unexpected return of a tyrant believed to be dead. In the first part of the play, the characters do not merely offer their viewpoints upon Herod's supposed death, but engage in courses of action in the light of it. Similarly, his return causes some characters to face the fatal consequences of their actions and others to choose further courses of action. As Nancy Gutierrez has pointed out, alongside the similarities, there are also considerable differences between *The Tragedy of Mariam* and the closet dramas of the Wilton circle:

> *Mariam* is surprisingly unlike the four closet dramas written earlier. The difference lies in the relationship between idea and plot. . . . The play is much more dramatic than its predecessors, in the sense that plot and character are served by idea rather than the other way around. (Gutierrez 242)

The generic categorisation of *The Tragedy of Mariam* as "closet" drama has meant that, until recently, the performance dimension of the play has either been ignored or worse, dismissed altogether.[10] However, critics have tended to make the mistake of considering "performance" per se to be synonymous with performance in the public theatre. Nancy Cotton's remark is revealing:

> [*Mariam*] was never intended for acting. Neither the Countess of Pembroke nor Viscountess Falkland wrote their plays for the stage; *Antonie and Mariam* were written as closet drama. To write for the public stage was déclassé. (Cotton 37)

Cotton conflates the public stage with all other arenas of dramatic production, from which she then excludes all aristocratic writers, male and female. Yet, when Cary was writing, the aristocracy was experiencing the apotheosis of that most theatrically self-conscious form of entertainment: the court masque. Anna of Denmark brought with her to the English court a sophisticated knowledge of the genre and, together with Inigo Jones, Ben Jonson and Samuel Daniel, staged dramatic fictions on a lavish scale. The public theatre was not the only playing space in Renaissance England.

Fortunately, in recent years, criticism on *The Tragedy of Mariam* has begun to notice the play's theatrical elements. Richard Levin and R.V. Holdsworth have noted the play's influence upon *A Fair Quarrel* (Levin 152-53) and *The Second Maiden's Tragedy* (Holdsworth 379-80). Cerasano and Wynne-Davies see similarities between Cary's Doris and Shakespeare's Queen Margaret in *Henry VI, Part I* (1591-92) and in *Richard III* (1593) and between Othello's unfounded jealousy and that of Herod. "*The Tragedy of Mariam*, therefore needs to be read, not only as addressing concerns particular to women, but as part of the overall development of Renaissance tragedy" (Cerasano and Wynne-Davies 10). Weller and Ferguson write: "The dramatic energy of Mariam makes the play seem more consonant with the popular stage than most 'closet dramas' are." They go on to claim the influence of Shakespearean dramaturgy, especially in Mariam's soliloquies, which

> go beyond the expository function they seem to serve in most earlier neoclassical drama; they represent the speaker's process of thought, her reflective and by no means static exploration of her own situation. (43)

Finally, Nancy Gutierrez makes a convincing argument for the crucial nature of the beholder's share in the dynamic of the play. Referring to its lack of closure, she writes:

> The rhetorical effect of such a structure is to ask for either assent or criticism from an audience that, together with the characters in the play, has observed and formed an opinion about the hero's actions. We might call this kind of closet drama a debate, in which the resolution of the plot is left open-ended, to be made complete by audience response. (Gutierrez 246)

Dismissing the play's status as a performance text has become increasingly difficult in the light of practical investigations into the play's performability. Small sections of *The Tragedy of Mariam* were included in "Attending to Renaissance Women," a performance scripted by Sharon Ammen and Catherine Schuler, and staged at the first Attending to Women in Early Modern England Conference in 1990.[11] The play proper was given its premiere by Tinderbox Theatre Co. at the Alhambra Studio, Bradford, England, in October 1994, directed by the present editor.[12] What became apparent from the rehearsal period and from the performance was that *The Tragedy of Mariam* is a play peopled by well-drawn characters, whose psychological complexity creates a drama which is variously horrifying, tense, and darkly comic. The Chorus was represented by two figures, a Gravedigger and a Sculptor, whose voices (both sung and spoken) emphasised the internal inconsistencies of the text. Costumed in modern dress, and performed on a set which included busts of Julius Caesar, Mark Antony and Octavius Caesar, the graves of Aristobolus and Hircanus, and a propagandist poster of Herod, the production had a successful five night run. The run included a matinee specially commissioned for an academic audience, followed by a discussion between audience and cast,[13] during which it became apparent that seeing the play in performance raised new and exciting questions. A second production, directed by Elizabeth Schafer and performed by students at Royal Holloway, took place in November 1995. In this production, all the parts were taken by women, with the exception of Antipater, who was played by a small boy. This was a thought-provoking decision, recreating the possible conditions of a private performance in the early seventeenth century. The historical context of pre-Christian Judea was the inspiration for the music, choreography and costumes of the main characters. The Chorus was presented as Elizabeth Cary herself, positioned in front of a portrait which represented the masculine authority of her husband. This controversial interpretation dealt with the problematic Chorus III by having the actor read most of it out of a book (presumably a conduct book), although the last two lines were delivered as Cary's own conclusion in the light of her reading. In 1996, English Alternative Theatre presented a staged reading of the play at the University of

Kansas, directed by Paul Stephen Lim, and with a script which had undergone some changes. Baba's sons were dropped, but Mariam's son became an on stage presence, presumably as a counterweight to Antipater, thereby making stronger parallels between Doris and Mariam. The fact that this play has received three radically different stagings in as many years is surely testimony to its power to signify as both literary and theatrical text.

The 1613 Edition

"The Tragedie of Mariam, the faire Queene of Jewry" was entered for publication in The Stationer's Register on 17 December 1612. It was published by Richard Hawkins and printed by Thomas Creede. In preparing this edition, I have located the following extant copies of the 1613 edition:

British Museum, shelfmark 162.c.28 – (A)
British Museum, shelfmark G.11221 – (B)
British Museum, shelfmark C.43.c.9 – (C)
National Library of Scotland, shelfmark Bute.58 – (D)
National Library of Scotland, shelfmark H.3.d.73 – (E)
National Library of Scotland, shelfmark Cwn.163 – (F)
Bodleian Library, shelfmark 4oT 35(2) Art. – (G)
Bodleian Library, shelfmark Mal.198(5) – (Bod.M)
Victoria & Albert Museum, Dyce Collection – (Dyce)
Eton College Library – (Eton)
The Shakespeare Birthplace Trust – (Sh.B)
Worcester College Library – (Wo)
Boston Public Library – (BP)
Elizabethan Club, Yale University – (EC)
Folger Shakespeare Library – (Fo)
Houghton Library, Harvard University – (Ho)
Huntington Library – (Hu)
Newberry Library – (N)
New York Public Library – (NY)

Pierpont Morgan Library – (PM)
Beinecke Library, Yale University – (Y)

I have been able to refer to all of the above, either in the original or in microfilm/photocopy format, except for the copy owned by the Boston Public Library, which, for insurance reasons, was unable to provide me with a copy.

Much of the groundwork in the collation of these copies has been done by Weller and Ferguson (43-47). However, in the preparation of their edition, they did not consult Sh.B and PM; nor did they note the substantial emendations to Bod.M. The most significant single variation between the extant texts is the absence of the leaf A1 from the majority of copies, and its presence only in the Huntington and Houghton. On A1^r is the Dedicatory Poem and on A1^v is the list of characters, "The Names of the Speakers". Dunstan (p. ix) assumed that this leaf had been added. However, as cancelled stubs are visible in Eton and Bod.M, the more likely explanation, put forward by Weller and Ferguson (44-45), is that A1 was removed once the play was put on public sale and those which were circulated within Cary's family and friends (and possibly at court) retained A1. Other textual variations are minimal:

Catchword of G1^v reads Youlle in A, D, BP, PM, Y
Catchword of G1^v reads Youl'e in B, C, E, F, G, Bod.M, Dyce, Eton, Sh.B, Wo, EC, Fo, Ho, Hu, N, NY,

Final word of IV vii . . . on G3^v reads a new in A, D, BP, PM, Y
Final word of IV vii . . . on G3^v reads anew in B, C, E, F, G, Bod.M, Dyce, Sh.B, Eton, Wo, EC, Fo, Ho, Hu, N, NY

Fourth word of V i . . . and second word of V i . . . on H4^v reads faine in A, D, F, G, Dyce, Wo, Ho, N, Y
Fourth word of V i . . . and second word of V i . . . on H4^v reads fame in B, C, E, Bod.M, Eton, SH.B, BP, EC, Fo, Hu, NY, PM

D is singular in that it retains the first word "I" on F3^r, which is missing in the other copies.

Most of the copies are complete, although the title page of B is mutilated and Sh.B lacks the title page, A4 and sig. I. C also lacks sig. I, although the missing section of the play has been supplied in MS by an unkown hand. Of perhaps more interest to the editor are the MS emendations which appear in many of the original copies. A, E, Bod.M, Dyce, Eton, Wo, PM, Fo, EC, Ho, Hu all contain at least one emendation. Because these are so numerous, varied and of considerable editorial significance, they have been cited in the list of Emendations and Variant Readings.

Notes

1. Newdigate (78) argues that because Drayton addresses Elizabeth as "My honoured Mistres" this suggests that he was in her father's employ. Drayton dedicated the epistles between William de la Pole, Duke of Suffolk, and Queen Margaret to Elizabeth Tanfield.

2. This biography, now housed in the Archives dèpartementales du Nord, Lille, was written by one of Elizabeth Cary's four daughters who entered the Convent of Cambrai between 1638 and 1639 and was probably written some time during the 1650s. As an historical source it is very useful, but needs to be viewed with caution due to its hagiographical tone and overriding concern to represent the progress of Elizabeth Cary's soul towards Catholicism.

3. The name "Graphina" was possibly suggested by the name of another character in *The Antiquities*, "Glaphyra," which appears on the same page as the story of Pheroras and his maidservant (*Ant.* 424). Graphina's name could also derive from the Greek for "writing." For a fuller discussion of the significance of

Graphina's name and character, see Margaret W. Ferguson, "Renaissance concepts of the 'woman writer,'" *Women and Literature in Britain 1500-1700*. Ed. Helen Wilcox. Cambridge: Cambridge University Press, 1996. 143-68.

4. Comparison with the court masque is an effective method of illustrating the extent to which Cary's re-working of her sources constitutes a radical comment upon contemporary ideology. The court masque displayed the beneficent rule of the father/King; in the early years of James VI and I's reign the court masque often focused upon his power to overcome unruly or unsightly women. For example, in Queen Anna's *Masque of Blackness*, 1605, the ladies appeared as blackamoors who experienced a vision which instructed them to seek for a land ending in -tania. This is Britannia:

> Ruled by a sun, that to this height doth grace it.
> Whose beams shine day and night, and are of force
> To blanch an Ethiop and revive a cor'se. (Lindley 6)

This celestial body is, of course, King James himself. Conversely, *The Tragedy of Mariam* presents us with the malevolent effects of a patriarch whose authority demands the death of those who are virtuous and fair (be they male or female). More subversively, this patriarch makes both necessary and possible the activation of otherwise dormant female forces of chaos and destruction.

5. See Belsey (174-75); Callaghan (173); Cotton (34); Dunstan (36); Fischer (234-35); Kennedy (120); Krontiris (85); Lewalski (196-97); Raber (335); Straznicky (127). Weller and Ferguson trace, via the Chorus, an implicit similarity between the two characters (36).

6. See Beilin (167); Ferguson (1992, 237-38); Kemp (458); Skura (29).

7. For further discussions of the Chorus, see Ferguson (240-44); Kennedy (121-29); Raber (326-29).

8. For a fuller discussion of the problematic nature of this term, see Alison Findlay, Stephanie Hodgson-Wright, and Gweno Williams, "'The Play is Ready to be Acted': Women and Dramatic Production 1550-1670," *Women's Writing: The Elizabethan to Victorian Period* 6:1 (1999): 129-48.

9. For different views, see Cerasano and Wynne-Davies (46-47); Gutierrez (326-28); Lewalski (200); Raber (325); Shannon (146); Straznicky (109).

10. "Perhaps influenced by the work of the Countess of Pembroke's coterie, or by her own reading of Seneca, Cary chose to write a classical play, a closet drama never intended for performance." (Beilin 62) "Stylistically and dramaturgically, the play is competently though conventionally Senecan. Action is discussed rather than dramatized . . . Cary uses the literarily varied prosody instead of the dramatically supple blank verse of her theatrical contemporaries." (Cotton 33); "her writing appeals to the intellect rather than to the emotions; *Mariam* was almost certainly intended for reading, rather than for acting, in the tradition of the dramas of the Pembroke group. And it is not actable." (Travitsky 215). Of the early critics, only Catherine Belsey supplies an appropriate caveat: "Elizabeth Cary's play, exploring the problem of a woman's right to speak, was a closet drama clearly not offered for performance – or certainly not for performance on the public stage." (Belsey 175). Most recently, Helen Hackett writes: "The 'closet' play, then, becomes its own speaking metaphor for the aristocratic married woman's access to public language, a form of verbal power that appears to sidestep the problem of women's speaking in public precisely because the play is not designed for performance." (Hackett 273)

11. The script was published in the conference proceedings, *Attending to Women in Early Modern England*, ed. Betty S. Travitsky and Adele Seef. London: Associated University Presses, 1994. 343-55.

12. For a fuller discussion of this production, see Alison Findlay, Stephanie Hodgson-Wright, and Gweno Williams, "(En)gendering Performance: Staging Plays by Early Modern Women," *Attending to Early Modern Women 1997.* Ed. Jane Donawerth and Adele Seef. Newark: University of Delaware Press (forthcoming).

13. The cast were: Sian Meyrick and Paula M. Wells (Chorus); Jo Dyer (Mariam); Lou Ford (Alexandra/Butler/Ananell); Suzannah Rogers (Salome); Paul Walker (Silleus); Anthony Bentley (Constabarus); Orazio Rea (Pheroras); Lyndsey Smith (Graphina/Nuntio); Andrew Maher (Baba's 1st Son/Sohemus); Graeme Watson (Baba's 2nd Son); Elizabeth Stannard (Doris); Robyn Howarth (Antipater); Dave Newport (Herod). Paula M. Wells set Chorus I, II and IV to original music.

Elizabeth Cary: A Brief Chronology

1585   Elizabeth Tanfield born at Burford Priory, Oxfordshire, to Lawrence Tanfield, a lawyer and later Lord Chief Justice, and Elizabeth Symondes of Norfolk.

1597   *England's Heroicall Epistles*, by Michael Drayton, published with a dedication to Elizabeth.

1598   Probable date of Cary's first extant work, *The Mirror of the World*, a manuscript translation of Abraham Ortelius' *Le Miroir du Monde*, dedicated to her maternal uncle, Sir Henry Lee.

1602   Elizabeth marries Sir Henry Cary, son of Sir Edward and Lady Katherine Cary of Berkhamstead, Hertfordshire.

1604   Probable date of Cary's first play, currently lost. Henry Cary travels to the Continent.

1606   Henry Cary returns to England.

1606-08 Probable date of *The Tragedy of Mariam*. Possible date of Cary's verse life of Tamburlaine, currently lost.

1609   Lucius Cary, Elizabeth's first child, born. Over the next fourteen years, Elizabeth gives birth to ten more children.

1612   *The Muses Sacrifice*, by Sir John Davies, published. Elizabeth is joint dedicatee, together with Mary, Dowager Countess of Pembroke and Lucy, Countess of Bedford.

1613   *The Tragedy of Mariam* published.

1614   Second edition of *England's Helicon* or *The Muses Harmony*, ed. John Bodenham, published with a dedication to Elizabeth.

1620   Henry Cary is created first Viscount Falkland.

1621   Elizabeth's and Henry's court portraits painted by Paul Van Somer.

1622   Elizabeth and Henry set sail for Ireland, where Henry is to take up his new post as Lord Deputy. Elizabeth allows Henry to mortgage her jointure in order to finance this journey, and is consequently disinherited by her father.

1625   Elizabeth returns to England. *A Sixth Book to the Countess of Pembroke's Arcadia*, by Richard Beling, published with a dedication to Elizabeth. Probable date of Cary's manuscript *Edward II: His Reign and Death. With the Fall of those Two his great Favourites, Gaveston and Spencer.* Two amended versions of this manuscript were published in 1680 as *The History of the Life, Reign and Death of Edward II* and *The History of the Most Unfortunate Prince King Edward II*, the first being attributed to an unnamed male author and the second to Henry Cary.

1626   Elizabeth converts to Catholicism. Henry withholds maintenance from Elizabeth, resulting in a protracted dispute involving letters and petitions to the King. From this time forward, Elizabeth is constantly short of money.

1629   Henry is recalled to England.

1630   Elizabeth's translation of Jacques Davy, Cardinal du Perron's *The Reply of the Most Illustrious Cardinal of Perron* published with a dedication to Queen Henrietta Maria.

1633   *The Works of John Marston*, ed. William Sheares, published
        with a dedication to Elizabeth. Henry Cary dies after a
        shooting accident at Theobald's Park.

1636   Elizabeth is accused of smuggling her two youngest sons,
        Patrick and Henry, to France to be received into the
        Catholic faith. She is examined by Lord Chief Justice
        Bramston and called before Star Chamber.

1638   Elizabeth's daughters, Lucy, Mary and Elizabeth are received
        into the Benedictine Convent at Cambrai, France.

1639   Elizabeth's daughter Anne is received into the Benedictine
        Convent at Cambrai, France.
        Elizabeth Cary dies in October and is buried in Henrietta
        Maria's private chapel.

A Note on the Text

All spelling and punctuation has been standardised and modernised. Where this has involved a substantial change from the original, the change has been noted in the list of Emendations and Variant Readings. Speakers' names have been given in full, as opposed to the varied abbreviations (e.g., Ma; Mar; Mari for Mariam) in the 1613 text. Act and scene numbers have been standardised to Roman numerals (e.g., I. i), replacing the Latin text of the original (e.g., Actus primus. Scoena prima). The stage directions of the 1613 text, although numerous, are inconsistent and occasionally unclear. Exits and entrances have been marked according to the requirements of the text and, as with the act and scene numbers, Latin text has been replaced with stage directions in English. As with spelling and punctuation, where this has involved a substantial change from the original, the change has been noted in the list of Emendations and Variant Readings.

T&HE TRAGEDIE

OF MARIAM,

THE FAIRE
Queene of Iewry.

Written by that learned,
vertuous, and truly noble Ladie,
E. C.

LONDON.
Printed by Thomas Creede, for Richard
Hawkins, and are to be folde at his shoppe
in Chancery Lane, neere vnto
Sargeants Inne.
1613.

TO DIANA'S EARTHLY DEPUTESS,
and my worthy sister,
Mistress Elizabeth Cary.[1]

When cheerful Phoebus[2] his full course hath run,
His sister's fainter beams our hearts doth cheer:
So your fair brother is to me the sun,
And you his sister as my moon appear.

You are my next belov'd, my second friend,   5
For when my Phoebus' absence makes it night,
Whilst to th'Antipodes his beams do bend,
From you my Phoebe,[3] shines my second light.

He like to Sol,[4] clear-sighted, constant, free;
You Luna-like,[5] unspotted, chaste, divine.   10
He shone on Sicily; you destined be,
T'illumine the now obscured Palestine.
My first was consecrated to Apollo,[6]
My second to Diana[7] now shall follow.

                                      E.C.

---

1   Dedicatory Sonnet: There are two possible identities of the Elizabeth Cary to
     whom the play is dedicated. The one cited by Dunstan (v-ix) is the author's sister-
     in-law, born Elizabeth Bland of Carleton, who married Henry's brother, Sir Philip
     in 1609. The other possible identity, cited by Weller and Ferguson (151) is Henry
     Cary's own sister Elizabeth, who was married to Sir John Savile in 1586. Although
     this marriage precedes the earliest date of the play's composition, i.e., 1602, it is
     possible that the author simply referred to her sister-in-law by her maiden title.
2   The Greek god of the sun.
3   The Greek goddess of the moon.
4   The sun.
5   The moon.
6   The Roman god of the sun.
7   The Roman goddess of the moon.

THE NAMES OF THE SPEAKERS

HEROD	King of Judea	
DORIS	His first wife	
MARIAM	His second wife	
SALOME	Herod's sister	
ANTIPATER	His son by Doris	5
ALEXANDRA	Mariam's mother	
SILLEUS	Prince of Arabia	
CONSTABARUS	Husband to Salome	
PHERORAS	Herod's brother	
GRAPHINA	His love	10
BABA'S FIRST SON		
BABA'S SECOND SON		
ANANELL	The high priest	
SOHEMUS	A counsellor to Herod	
NUNTIO	A messenger	15
BUTLER	Another messenger	
CHORUS	A company of Jews	
SILLEUS' MAN		
SOLDIERS		
ATTENDANTS		

THE ARGUMENT[1]

Herod, the son of Antipater (an Idumean)[2] having crept, by the favour of the Romans, into the Jewish monarchy, married Mariam the daughter[3] of Hircanus,[4] the rightful King and priest, and for her (besides her high blood, being of singular beauty) he repudiated Doris, his former wife, by whom he 5 ~~denied~~
~~the truth~~
~~of~~
had children.

This Mariam had a brother called Aristobolus, and next him and Hircanus his grandfather, Herod in his wife's right had the best title. Therefore to remove them, he charged the first with treason and put him to death; and drowned the second under 10 colour of sport.[5] Alexandra, daughter to the one, and mother to the other, accused him for their deaths before Antony.[6]

So when he was forced to go answer this accusation at Rome, he left the custody of his wife to Josephus, his uncle, that had married his sister Salome, and out of a violent affection 15 (unwilling any should enjoy her after him) he gave strict and private commandment that if he were slain, she should be put to death. But he returned with much honour, yet found his wife extremely discontented, to whom Josephus had (meaning it for the best, to prove Herod loved her) revealed his charge. 20

So by Salome's accusation he put Josephus to death, but was reconciled to Mariam, who still bore the death of her friends exceeding hardly.

---

1   This was printed on the back of the leaf bearing the Dedicatory Poem. The Eton copy contains a MS dramatis personae, split into male characters and female characters. It is of particular interest as it includes those not listed in 1613.
2   Literally, a native of Idumea. The term also denotes the descendants of Esau, alternatively called Edom, who founded the land of Idumea. They were not considered to be true Jews as they were not descended from Jacob. Therefore, the term is employed pejoratively by Mariam and Alexandra to refer to Herod and his family.
3   Properly, granddaughter.
4   John Hircanus, last of the Hasmonean kings.
5   The manner of the two deaths is reversed. In fact, Herod accused Hircanus of treason and arranged to have Aristobolus drowned in a fake accident.
6   Mark Antony (c. 82-30 BC).

In this mean time Herod was again necessarily to revisit Rome, for Caesar[1] having overthrown Antony, his great friend 25 was likely to make an alteration of his fortune.

In his absence, news came to Jerusalem that Caesar had put him to death. Their willingness it should be so, together with the likelihood, gave this rumour so good credit as Sohemus that had suceeded in Josephus' charge, succeeded him likewise 30 in revealing it. So at Herod's return which was speedy and unexpected, he found Mariam so far from joy, that she showed apparent signs of sorrow. He still desiring to win her to a better humour; she being very unable to conceal her passion, fell to upbraiding him with her brother's death. As they were thus 35 debating, came in a fellow with a cup of wine, who, hired by Salome, said first it was a love potion, which Mariam desired to deliver to the King; but afterwards he affirmed that it was a poison, and that Sohemus had told her somewhat which procured the vehement hate in her. 35

The King hearing this, more moved with jealousy of Sohemus, than with this intent of poison, sent her away and presently after by the instigation of Salome, she was beheaded. Which rashness was afterward punished in him, with an intolerable and almost frantic passion for her death.

---

1   Octavius Caesar (63 BC-AD 14), later known as the emperor Caesar Augustus, who defeated Mark Antony at the battle of Actium.

ACT I

Scene i

(Enter Mariam)

MARIAM. How oft have I, with public voice run on
To censure Rome's last hero¹ for deceit?
Because he wept when Pompey's life was gone,
Yet when he lived, he thought his name too great.
But now I do recant and, Roman lord,   5
Excuse too rash a judgement in a woman:
My sex pleads pardon, pardon then afford,
Mistaking is with us but too, too common.
Now do I find by self experience taught,
One object yields both grief and joy.   10
You wept indeed when on his worth you thought,
But joyed that slaughter did your foe destroy.
So at his death your eyes true drops did rain,
Whom dead, you did not wish alive again.
When Herod lived, that now is done to death,   15
Oft have I wished that I from him were free,
Oft have I wished that he might lose his breath,
Oft have I wished his carcass dead to see.
Then rage and scorn had put my love to flight,
That love which once on him was firmly set;   20
Hate hid his true affection from my sight,
And kept my heart from paying him his debt.
And blame me not, for Herod's jealousy
Had power ev'n constancy itself to change:
For he by barring me from liberty,   25
To shun my ranging, taught me first to range.²

---

1   Weller and Ferguson (153) suggest that the reference is to Julius Caesar's reaction
    to the dead Pompey's severed head, detailed in Plutarch's *Lives*.
2   Herod's restrictions upon Mariam proved counterproductive in that they made
    her wish for more freedom than she might otherwise have desired.

But yet too chaste a scholar was my heart
To learn to love another than my lord;
To leave his love, my lesson's former part,
I quickly learned, the other I abhorred.[1]   30
But now his death to memory doth call
The tender love that he to Mariam bore,
And mine to him. This makes those rivers fall,
Which by another thought unmoist'nèd are.
For Aristobolus, the loveliest youth   35
That ever did in angel's shape appear,
The cruel Herod was not moved to ruth,[2]
Then why grieves Mariam Herod's death to hear?
Why joy I not the tongue no more shall speak
That yielded forth my brother's latest doom?   40
Both youth and beauty might thy fury break,
And both in him did ill befit a tomb.
And, worthy grandsire, ill did he requite
His high ascent, alone by thee procured,
Except he murdered thee to free the sprite[3]   45
Which still he thought on earth too long immured.
How happy was it that Sohemus' mind
Was moved to pity my distressed estate?
Might Herod's life a trusty servant find,
My death to his had been unseparate.   50
These thoughts have power his death to make me bear;
Nay more, to wish the news may firmly hold.
Yet cannot this repulse some falling tear
That will against my will some grief unfold.
And more I owe him for his love to me,   55
The deepest love that ever yet was seen;
Yet had I rather much a milkmaid be,
Than be the monarch of Judea's Queen.
It was for nought but love he wished his end

---

1 Mariam could easily reject Herod, but could not commit adultery with another man.
2 Pity.
3 Soul, spirit.

Might to my death but the vaunt-courier[1] prove.   60
But I had rather still be foe than friend
To him that saves for hate and kills for love.
Hard-hearted Mariam! At thy discontent,
What floods of tears have drenched his manly face?
How canst thou then so faintly now lament   65
Thy truest lover's death, a death's disgrace?
Aye, now mine eyes you do begin to right
The wrongs of your admirer and my lord.
Long since you should have put your smiles to flight!
Ill doth a widowed eye with joy accord.   70
Why now methinks the love I bore him then,
When virgin freedom left me unrestrained,
Doth to my heart begin to creep again:
My passion now is far from being feigned.
But tears fly back and hide you in your banks,   75
You must not be to Alexandra seen,
For if my moan be spied, but little thanks
Shall Mariam have from that incensèd Queen.

Scene ii

(Enter Alexandra)

ALEXANDRA. What means these tears? My Mariam doth mistake.
The news we heard did tell the tyrant's end!
What, weepst thou for thy brother's murd'rer's sake?
Will ever wight[2] a tear for Herod spend?
My curse pursue his breathless trunk and spirit,   5
Base Edomite,[3] the damnèd Esau's heir.
Must he ere[4] Jacob's child[5] the crown inherit?

---

1 A messenger sent to prepare the way or announce the arrival of another.
2 Living creature.
3 One descended from Esau, therefore not a true Jew.
4 Before.
5 A descendant of Jacob, in this case Alexandra's progeny.

Must he, vile wretch, be set in David's chair?[1]
No, David's soul, within the bosom placed
Of our forefather Abram, was ashamed   10
To see his seat with such a toad disgraced,
That seat that hath by Judah's race been famed.
Thou fatal enemy to royal blood,
Did not the murder of my boy suffice
To stop thy cruel mouth that gaping stood,   15
But must thou dim the mild Hircanus' eyes?
My gracious father, whose too ready hand
Did lift this Idumean from the dust.
And he, ungrateful caitiff,[2] did withstand
The man that did in him most friendly trust.   20
What kingdom's right could cruel Herod claim?
Was he not Esau's issue, heir of hell?
Then what succession can he have but shame?
Did not his ancestor his birth-right sell?
O yes, he doth from Edom's name derive   25
His cruel nature, which with blood is fed.
That made him me of sire and son deprive;
He ever thirsts for blood, and blood is red.[3]
Weepst thou because his love to thee was bent?
And readst thou love in crimson characters?   30
Slew he thy friends to work thy heart's content?
No, hate may justly call that action hers.
He gave the sacred priesthood for thy sake
To Aristobolus, yet doomed him dead
Before his back the ephod[4] warm could make,   35

---

1   The throne of Judea.
2   Someone base and wretched.
3   Esau sold his birthright to his brother Jacob for a red stew of venison, for which he
    craved (Genesis 25:29-34, *Geneva*). The name Edom means "red stuff" and became
    an alternative name for Esau, because of his craving. Herod, like his ancestor, craves
    for red stuff, but unlike his ancestor, craves for blood rather than venison stew.
4   Jewish priestly garment, without sleeves, slit at the sides below the armpits and
    fastened with buckles at the shoulders and a girdle at the waist. The high priest's
    was brightly coloured, of gold, purple and scarlet.

And ere the mitre[1] settled on his head.
Oh, had he given my boy no less than right,
The double oil[2] should to his forehead bring
A double honour, shining doubly bright:
His birth anointed him both priest and King.   40
And say my father and my son he slew,
To royalize, by right your prince-born breath;
Was love the cause, can Mariam deem it true,
That Herod gave commandment for her death?
I know by fits, he showed some signs of love,   45
And yet not love, but raging lunacy,
And this his hate to thee may justly prove
That sure he hates Hircanus' family.
Who knows if he, unconstant wavering lord,
His love to Doris had renewed again   50
And that he might his bed to her afford?
Perchance he wished that Mariam might be slain?
MARIAM.   Doris? Alas her time of love was past,
    Those coals were raked in embers long ago,
    If Mariam's love, and she, was now disgraced.   55
    Nor did I glory in her overthrow.
    He not a whit his first born son esteemed,
    Because as well as his he was not mine:
    My children only for his own he deemed.
    These boys that did descend from royal line,   60
    These did he style his heirs to David's throne.
    My Alexander, if he live, shall sit
    In the majestic seat of Solomon.[3]
    To will it so, did Herod think it fit.
ALEXANDRA.   Why? Who can claim from Alexander's brood   65
    That gold-adornèd lion-guarded chair?
    Was Alexander not of David's blood?

---

1   Ceremonial turban of the high priest.
2   Oil was used for anointing both kings and priests (1 Samuel 11; Leviticus 8, *Geneva*).
    Aristobolus, as well as being high priest, was also rightful heir to the throne.
3   King of Judea, famed for his wisdom.

And was not Mariam Alexander's heir?[1]
What more than right could Herod then bestow?
And who will think, except for more than right?'   70
He did not raise them, for they were not low,
But born to wear the crown in his despite.[2]
Then send those tears away that are not sent
To thee by reason, but by passion's power.
Thine eyes to cheer, thy cheeks to smiles be bent,   75
And entertain with joy this happy hour.
Felicity,[3] if when she comes, she finds
A mourning habit and a cheerless look,
Will think she is not welcome to thy mind,
And so perchance her lodging will not brook.   80
Oh keep her whilst thou hast her; if she go
She will not easily return again.
Full many a year have I endured in woe,
Yet still have sued her presence to obtain.
And did not I to her as presents send   85
A table,[4] that best art did beautify
Of two, to whom Heaven did best feature lend,
To woo her love by winning Antony?
For when a prince's favour we do crave,
We first their minions' loves do seek to win.   90
So I, that sought Felicity to have,
Did with her minion Antony begin.

---

1   The references to "Alexander" are confusing. Both Mariam's son and father were
    called Alexander, and so the Alexander of whom Mariam speaks is her son,
    whereas Alexandra is speaking of her husband, Mariam's father.
2   Everyone will be of the opinion that Mariam's son is the rightful heir due to his
    birth, Mariam being a direct descendent of David, rather than being named as
    heir by Herod.
3   The personification of good fortune.
4   A board on which portraits were painted. This refers to the occasion on which
    Alexandra sent portraits of Aristobolus and Mariam to Antony, hoping that their
    beauty would attract his favour. Josephus (*Ant.*, 386), suggests that Antony was
    equally attracted to the siblings, and on hearing that Mariam was already married
    to Herod sent for Aristobolus. Herod, fearing that Aristobolus' influence over
    Antony might adversely affect his own position, prevented Aristobolus from going.

With double sleight I sought to captivate
The warlike lover, but I did not right.
For if my gift had borne but half the rate,[1]   95
The Roman had been over-taken quite.
But now he farèd like a hungry guest,
That to some plenteous festival is gone;
Now this, now that, he deems to eat were best,
Such choice doth make him let them all alone.   100
The boy's large forehead first did fairest seem,
Then glanced his eye upon my Mariam's cheek,
And that without comparison did deem.
What was in either, but he most did seek,
And thus distracted, either's beauties might   105
Within the other's excellence was drowned:
Too much delight did bar him from delight,
For either's love, the other's did confound.
Where if thy portraiture had only gone,
His life from Herod, Antony had taken.   110
He would have loved thee, and thee alone,
And left the brown Egyptian clean forsaken.
And Cleopatra then to seek had been
So firm a lover of her wanèd face;
Then great Antonius' fall we had not seen,   115
By her that fled to have him hold the chase.[2]
Then Mariam in a Roman's chariot set,
In place of Cleopatra might have shown
χ A mart[3] of beauties in her visage met,
And part in this, that they were all her own.   120
MARIAM.   Not to be Empress of aspiring Rome,
     Would Mariam like to Cleopatra live:

---

1   Value.
2   A reference to Cleopatra's tactics at Actium, 31 BC. Her ship fled from the battle,
    Antony followed, and thus lost the battle to Octavius Caesar.
3   Market, display of goods. The commercial allusion is particularly appropriate in this
χ   context. The next line refers to Cleopatra's use of make-up. Mariam's "mart of beauty"
    is superior to Cleopatra's because it is natural ("her own") rather than painted on.

With purest body will I press my tomb,
And wish no favours Antony could give.

ALEXANDRA. Let us retire us, that we may resolve   125
How now to deal in this reversèd state.
Great are th'affairs that we must now revolve,[1]
And great affairs must not be taken late.

Scene iii

(Enter Salome)

SALOME. More plotting yet? Why? Now you have the thing
For which so oft you spent your suppliant breath.
And Mariam hopes to have another king,
Her eyes do sparkle joy for Herod's death.

ALEXANDRA. If she desired another king to have,   5
She might, before she came in Herod's bed,
Have had her wish. More kings than one did crave
For leave to set a crown upon her head.
I think with more than reason she laments
That she is freed from such a sad annoy.   10
Who is't will weep to part from discontent?
And if she joy, she did not causeless joy.

SALOME. You durst not thus have given your tongue the rein,
If noble Herod still remained in life.
Your daughter's betters far, I dare maintain,   15
Might have rejoiced to be my brother's wife.

MARIAM. My betters far? Base woman, 'tis untrue.
You scarce have ever my superiors seen,
For Mariam's servants were as good as you,
Before she came to be Judea's Queen.   20

---

1   Consider. The next line confirms the urgent need for the women to turn their
    attention to the affairs of state.

SALOME. Now stirs the tongue that is so quickly moved,
    But more than once your choler[1] have I borne.
    Your fumish[2] words are sooner said than proved,
    And Salome's reply is only scorn.
MARIAM. Scorn those that are for thy companions held!   25
    Though I thy brother's face had never seen,
    My birth thy baser birth so far excelled,
    I had to both of you the Princess been.
    Thou parti-Jew, and parti-Edomite,[3]
    Thou mongrel, issued from rejected race!   30
    Thy ancestors against the heavens did fight,[4]
    And thou like them wilt heavenly birth disgrace.
SALOME. Still twit[5] you me with nothing but my birth?
    What odds betwixt your ancestors and mine?
    Both born of Adam, both were made of earth,   35
    And both did come from holy Abr'ham's line.
MARIAM. I favour thee when nothing else I say.
    With thy black acts I'll not pollute my breath,
    Else to thy charge I might full justly lay
    A shameful life, besides a husband's death.   40
SALOME. 'Tis true indeed, I did the plots reveal,
    That passed betwixt your favourites and you.
    I meant not I, a traitor to conceal,
    Thus Salome your minion Joseph slew.
MARIAM. Heaven, dost thou mean this infamy to smother?   45
    Let slandered Mariam ope thy closèd ear.
    Self-guilt hath ever been suspicion's mother,

---

1 Anger.
2 Irascible, inflammatory.
3 Mariam is referring to Salome's descent. As an Idumean (or Edomite) she was not
   born of true Jewish stock and yet she, like her brother Herod, was a Jew by faith.
4 Edom's conflict with Israel was considered by the Old Testament prophets to
   contravene and challenge divine will: "And the house of Iaakob shalbe a fyre and
   the house of Ioseph a flame, and the house of Esau as stubble, & thei shal kindle in them and devoure them: and there shal be no remnant of the house of
   Esau: for the Lord hathe spoken it" (Obadiah 1:21, *Geneva*).
5 Taunt.

And therefore I this speech with patience bear.
No, had not Salome's unsteadfast heart
In Joseph's stead her Constabarus placed,   50
To free herself she had not used the art
To slander hapless Mariam for unchaste.
ALEXANDRA.   Come Mariam, let us go: it is no boot[1] /
To let the head contend against the foot.   /

(Exeunt Mariam, Alexandra)

Scene iv

SALOME.   Lives Salome to get so base a style[2]
As foot to the proud Mariam? Herod's spirit
In happy time for her endured exile,[3]
For did he live she should not miss her merit.[4]
But he is dead, and though he were my brother,   5
His death such store of cinders cannot cast
My coals of love to quench, for though they smother
The flames a while, yet will they out at last.
Oh blessed Arabia, in best climate placed!
I by the fruit will censure of the tree: 10
'Tis not in vain, thy happy name thou hast,
If all Arabians like Silleus be.
Had not my fate been too, too contrary,
When I on Constabarus first did gaze,
Silleus had been object to mine eye,   15
Whose looks and personage must all eyes amaze.
But now ill fated Salome, thy tongue
To Constabarus by itself is tied,
And now, except I do the Hebrew wrong

---

1   No use.
2   Title, name.
3   Luckily for Mariam, Herod is dead.
4   "That which is deserved or has been earned, whether good or evil; due reward or punishment" (*OED*).

I cannot be the fair Arabian's bride.   20
What childish lets[1] are these? Why stand I now
On honourable points?[2] 'Tis long ago
Since shame was written on my tainted brow,[3]
And certain 'tis that shame is honour's foe.
Had I upon my reputation stood,   25
Had I affected an unspotted life,
Josephus' veins had still been stuffed with blood,
And I to him had lived a sober wife.
Then had I never cast an eye of love
On Constabarus' now detested face,   30
Then had I kept my thoughts without remove,[4]
And blushed at motion[5] of the least disgrace.
But shame is gone and honour wiped away,
And impudency on my forehead sits.
She bids me work my will without delay,   35
And for my will I will employ my wits.
He loves, I love. What then can be the cause
Keeps me from being the Arabian's wife?
It is the principles of Moses' laws,[6]
For Constabarus still remains in life.   40
If he to me did bear as earnest hate
As I to him, for him there were an ease:
A separating bill[7] might free his fate
From such a yoke that did so much displease.
Why should such privilege to men be given?   45

---

1 Hindrances.
2 "Standing upon points" meant adhering to a strict code of personal behaviour.
3 In Renaissance England, the brow or forehead was commonly viewed as indicative
   of a person's character. Cary makes sustained reference to this throughout the play.
4 Persuade away from purpose or resolve.
5 Emotion or impulse.
6 As Salome goes on to say, divorce was a male privilege under Mosaic Law: "If so
   be she finde no favour in his eyes, because he hath espied some filthiness in her,
   then let him write her a bil of divorcement" (Deuteronomy 24:1-4, *Geneva*). Of
   course, this could be interpreted in many different ways, which is the source of
   Doris' complaint in II. iii and IV. viii.
7 Legally binding document of divorce.

Or given to them, why barred from women then?
Are men than we in greater grace with heaven?
Or cannot women hate as well as men?
I'll be the custom-breaker, and begin
To show my sex the way to freedom's door.   50
And with an off'ring will I purge my sin –
The law was made for none but who are poor.
If Herod had lived, I might to him accuse
My present lord. But for the future's sake,[1]
Then would I tell the King he did refuse   55
The sons of Baba[2] in his power to take.
But now I must divorce him from my bed,
That my Silleus may possess his room.
Had I not begged his life he had been dead,[3]
I curse my tongue the hind'rer of his doom.   60
But then my wand'ring heart to him was fast,[4]
Nor did I dream of change. Silleus said
He would be here, and see he comes at last:
Had I not named him longer had he stayed.

---

1   This line is difficult both to interpret and to punctuate. The interpretation given here is
    that Salome is telling the audience that, if Herod were still alive, she could accuse Con-
    stabarus of treason and have him executed. However, that problematic phrase "But for the
    future's sake" I have taken as referring back to her earlier promise to get a divorce and so
    show women "the way to freedom's door." In other words, although having Constabarus
    executed may be easier for Salome herself, she also gives some thought to the potentially
    advantageous effect of setting a precedent for women to claim the right of divorce. This
    is all academic, of course, as Herod returns and Salome is forced to take the option of
    having Constabarus executed. Weller and Ferguson (159) offer a less complex reading
    – for the sake of her future husband she would, without hesitation, tell Herod.
2   Herod ordered Constabarus to capture and execute the sons of Baba. Constabarus,
    however, decided to offer them protection in hiding. The play presents his
    motives as entirely altruistic, although Josephus (*Ant.*, 400-01) describes his
    actions as resulting purely from self-interest. When the play opens, Constabarus
    has been hiding the sons of Baba for twelve years.
3   According to Josephus (*Ant.*, 400), whilst Constabarus was governor of Idumea,
    he tried to gain independence from Herod and Judea, by asking Cleopatra to get
    the kingdom from Antony. When Herod learned of Constabarus' duplicity, only
    the entreaties of Salome kept him from condemning Constabarus to death.
4   Fixed.

Scene v

(Enter Silleus)

SILLEUS.   Well found fair Salome, Judea's pride!
    Hath thy innated[1] wisdom found the way
    To make Silleus deem him deified,
    By gaining thee, O more than precious, pray?
SALOME.   I have devised the best I can devise,   5
    A more imperfect means was never found,
    But what cares Salome? It doth suffice
    If our endeavours with their end be crowned.
    In this our land we have an ancient use,
    Permitted first by our law-giver's head:[2]   10
    Who hates his wife, though for no just abuse,
    May with a bill divorce her from his bed.
    But in this custom women are not free,
    Yet I for once will wrest[3] it. Blame not thou
    The ill I do, since what I do's for thee.   15
    Though others blame, Silleus should allow.
SILLEUS.   Thinks Salome Silleus hath a tongue
    To censure her fair actions? Let my blood
    Bedash my proper[4] brow, for such a wrong,
    The being yours, can make even vices good.   20
    Arabia joy! Prepare thy earth with green!
    Thou never happy wert indeed till now!
    Now shall thy ground be trod by beauty's Queen,
    Her foot is destined to depress thy brow.
    Thou shalt, fair Salome, command as much   25
    As if the royal ornament were thine:
    The weakness of Arabia's King is such,
    The kingdom is not his so much as mine.

---

1   Innate, inherent.
2   Moses.
3   Force.
4   Own.

My mouth is our Obodas'[1] oracle,
Who thinks not aught but what Silleus will.   30
And thou rare creature, Asia's miracle,
Shalt be to me as it: Obodas still.

SALOME.   'Tis not for glory I thy love accept;
Judea yields me honour's worthy store.
Had not affection in my bosom crept,   35
My native country should my life deplore.[2]
Were not Silleus he with whom I go,
I would not change my Palestine for Rome.
Much less would I, a glorious state to show,
Go far to purchase an Arabian tomb.   40

SILLEUS.   Far be it from Silleus so to think.
I know it is thy gratitude[3] requites
The love that is in me, and shall not shrink
Till death do sever me from earth's delights.

SALOME.   But whist! Methinks the wolf is in our talk.[4]   45
Be gone Silleus. Who doth here arrive?
'Tis Constabarus that doth hither walk.
I'll find a quarrel, him from me to drive.

SILLEUS.   Farewell. But were it not for thy command,
In his despite Silleus here would stand.   *(Exit)*   50

Scene vi

(Enter Constabarus)

CONSTABARUS.   Oh Salome, how much you wrong your name,
Your race, your country, and your husband most.
A stranger's private conference is shame;

---

1   The slothful king of Arabia, described by Josephus (*Ant.*, 425).
2   Grieve over; despair of. Salome is saying that she would offend her "native country,"
    Palestine (i.e., it would despair of her), if she left it for any other reason than love.
3   Favour, grace. This meaning is chiefly Scottish and now obsolete (*OED*).
4   Hush, someone unpleasant is lurking nearby and listening.

ᵪ I blush for you, that have your blushing lost.
Oft have I found, and found you to my grief,   5
Consorted with this base Arabian here.
Heaven knows that you have been my comfort chief;
Then do not now my greater plague appear.
Now by the stately carvèd edifice,[1]
That on Mount Sion makes so fair a show,   10
And by the altar fit for sacrifice,
I love thee more than thou thyself dost know.
Oft with a silent sorrow have I heard
How ill Judea's mouth doth censure thee,
And did I not thine honour much regard,   15
Thou shouldst not be exhorted[2] thus for me.
Didst thou but know the worth of honest fame,
How much a virtuous woman is esteemed,
Thou wouldst like hell eschew deservèd shame,
And seek to be both chaste and chastely deemed.   20
Our wisest Prince[3] did say, and true he said,
A virtuous woman crowns her husband's head.

SALOME.   Did I for this uprear thy low estate?
Did I for this requital beg thy life,
That thou hadst forfeited to hapless fate,   25
To be to such a thankless wretch the wife?
This hand of mine hath lifted up thy head,
Which many a day ago had fallen full low,
Because the sons of Baba are not dead;
To me thou dost both life and fortune owe.   30

---

1   The fortress of Jerusalem and a place of sacred ceremony: "David toke the forte
    of Zion: this is the city of David" (2 Samuel 5:7, *Geneva*).
2   Admonished for wrongdoing; persuaded to better conduct. The syntax is a little
    peculiar in this line. The phrase "exhorted thus for me" suggests that the party
    doing the exhorting is not Constabarus, but "Judea's mouth" (14). Constabarus
    sanctimoniously implies that the people of Judea urge Salome toward better
    wifely behaviour for his sake and that he is complicit with such public exhortation,
    not for his own self-interest, but for the sake of Salome's moral welfare.
3   Solomon. Constabarus is referring to "A verteous woman is the crowne of her
    housband: but she that maketh him ashamed, is as a corruption in his bones"
    (Proverbs 12:4, *Geneva*).

CONSTABARUS. You have my patience often exercised,
  Use makes my choler keep within the banks,[1]
  Yet boast no more, but be by me advised:
  A benefit upbraided, forfeits thanks.
  I prithee Salome dismiss this mood,　　　　　　　35
  Thou dost not know how ill it fits thy place.
  My words were all intended for thy good,
  To raise thine honour and to stop disgrace.
SALOME. To stop disgrace? Take thou no care for me.
  Nay do thy worst, thy worst I set not by.　　　　40
  No shame of mine is like to light on thee,
  Thy love and admonitions I defy.
  Thou shalt no hour longer call me wife.
  Thy jealousy procures my hate so deep
  That I from thee do mean to free my life,　　　　45
  By a divorcing bill before I sleep.
CONSTABARUS. Are Hebrew women now transformed to men?
  Why do you not as well our battles fight
  And wear our armour? Suffer this, and then
  Let all the world be topsy-turvèd quite.　　　　50
  Let fishes graze, beasts swim, and birds descend,
  Let fire burn downwards whilst the earth aspires,
  Let winter's heat and summer's cold offend,
  Let thistles grow on vines, and grapes on briers.
  Set us to spin or sow, or at the best,　　　　　55
  Make us wood-hewers, water-bearing wights,
  For sacred service let us take no rest,
  Use us as Joshua did the Gibonites.[2]
SALOME. Hold on your talk till it be time to end!
  For me, I am resolved it shall be so.　　　　　60

---

1 Constabarus is so used to Salome's behaviour that he can easily stay calm in the
   face of her abuse.
2 The Gibonites were captured by Joshua who promised them harsh treatment:
   "Now therefore are ye cursed, and shal non of you be freed from being bondmen,
   and hewers of wood and drawers of water for the house of my God" (Joshua
   9:23, *Geneva*).

Though I be first that to this course do bend,
I shall not be the last, full well I know.
CONSTABARUS.	Why then be witness heav'n, the judge of sins,
Be witness spirits that eschew the dark,
Be witness angels, witness cherubins,	65
Whose semblance sits upon the holy Ark,[1]
Be witness earth, be witness Palestine,
Be witness David's city, if my heart
Did ever merit such an act of thine.
Or if the fault by mine that makes us part,	70
Since mildest Moses, friend unto the Lord,
Did work his wonders in the land of Ham,[2]
And slew the first-born babes without a sword,
In sign whereof we eat the holy lamb;
Till now that fourteen hundred years are past,	75
Since first the law with us hath been in force,
You are the first, and will, I hope, be last,
That ever sought her husband to divorce!
SALOME.	I mean not to be led by precedent,
My will shall be to me instead of law.	80
CONSTABARUS.	I fear me much you will too late repent
That you have ever lived so void of awe.
This is Silleus' love that makes you thus
Reverse all order. You must next be his.
But if my thoughts aright the cause discuss,[3]	85
In winning you, he gains no lasting bliss.
I was Silleus, and not long ago
Josephus then was Constabarus now:

1	The Ark of the Covenant, which held the two tablets of stone on which were written the Ten Commandments.
2	Egypt. The Egyptians were thought to be descended from Noah's second son, Ham, or Cham. Moses led the Israelites from their captivity in Egypt. The ten plagues were instrumental in the escape of the Israelites, the last one being the death of the first born, which "passed over" the dwellings of the Israelites and only affected the Egyptians. Eating the holy lamb refers to the celebration of the Passover.
3	If I surmise correctly.

When you became my friend you proved his foe,
As now for him you break to me your vow.[1]   90
SALOME.   If once I loved you, greater is your debt,
For certain 'tis that you deserved it not.
And undeservèd love we soon forget,
And therefore that to me can be no blot.
But now fare ill my once belovèd lord,   95
Yet never more beloved than now abhorred.   *(Exit)*
CONSTABARUS.   Yet Constabarus biddeth thee farewell.
Farewell light creature, Heaven forgive thy sin!
My prophesying spirit doth foretell
Thy wavering thoughts do yet but new begin.   100
Yet I have better 'scaped than Joseph did.
But if our Herod's death had been delayed,
The valiant youths that I so long have hid,
Had been by her, and I for them betrayed.
Therefore in happy hour did Caesar give   105
The fatal blow to wanton Antony,
For had he lived, our Herod then should live,
But great Antonius' death made Herod die.
Had he enjoyed his breath, not I alone
Had been in danger of a deadly fall,   110
But Mariam had the way of peril gone,
Though by the tyrant most beloved of all.
The sweet faced Mariam as free from guilt
As heaven from spots! Yet had her lord come back
Her purest blood had been unjustly spilt,   115
And Salome it was would work her wrack.[2]
Though all Judea yield her innocent,
She often hath been near to punishment.   *(Exit)*

---

1   The masculine pronouns "his" and "him" refer, respectively, to Salome's previous
      husband, Josephus, and to her intended husband, Silleus.
2   Destruction.

CHORUS.

Those minds that wholly dote upon delight,
Except[1] they only joy in inward good,
Still hope at last to hop upon the right,
And so from sand they leap in loathsome mud.
  Fond[2] wretches, seeking what they cannot find,   5
  For no content attends a wavering mind.

If wealth they do desire, and wealth attain,
Then wondrous fain[3] would they to honour leap.
If mean degree they do in honour gain,
They would but wish a little higher step.   10
  Thus step to step, and wealth to wealth they add,
  Yet cannot all their plenty make them glad.

Yet oft we see that some in humble state,
Are cheerfull, pleasant, happy and content,
When those indeed that are of higher state,   15
With vain additions do their thoughts torment.
  Th'one would to his mind his fortune bind,
  Th'other to his fortune frames his mind.

To wish variety is sign of grief,
For if you like your state as now it is,   20
Why should an alteration bring relief?
Nay, change would then be feared as loss of bliss.
  That man is only happy in his fate,
  That is delighted in a settled state.

---

1 Unless.
2 Foolish.
3 Rather.

Still Mariam wished she from her lord were free,   25
For expectation of variety.[1]
Yet now she sees her wishes prosperous be,
She grieves, because her lord so soon did die.
　　Who can those vast imaginations feed,
　　Where in a property, contempt doth breed?[2]   30

Were Herod now perchance to live again,
She would again as much be grieved at that.
All that she may, she ever doth disdain,
Her wishes guide her to she knows not what.
　　And sad must be their looks, their honour sour,   35
　　That care for nothing being in their power.

1　Weller and Ferguson (160) interpret the beginning of this stanza thus: "The
　　Chorus imputes to Mariam motives similar to Salome's described by
　　Constabarus." However, in the context of the Chorus, which chides humankind
　　for ever desiring a change in its state, it is more likely that the line means
　　"Mariam often wished to be free of Herod but never expected to be," the phrase
　　"for expectation of variety" referring to Mariam expecting her state to be variant
　　from what she wished, rather than to her desire for a multitude of lovers, a
　　motive from which Mariam has already distanced herself in I. i.
2　"Familiarity breeds contempt."

ACT II

Scene i

(Enter Pheroras and Graphina)

PHERORAS. 'Tis true Graphina, now the time draws nigh
   Wherein the holy priest with hallowed rite,
   The happy long-desirèd knot shall tie,
   Pheroras and Graphina to unite.
   How oft have I with lifted hands implored   5
   This blessèd hour, till now implored in vain,
   Which hath my wishèd liberty restored,
   And made my subject self my own again?
   Thy love, fair maid, upon mine eye doth sit,
   Whose nature hot doth dry the moisture all,   10
   Which were, in nature and in reason, fit
   For my monarchal brother's death to fall.
   Had Herod lived, he would have plucked my hand
   From fair Graphina's palm perforce, and tied
   The same in hateful and despisèd band,   15
   For I had had a baby to my bride.[1]
   Scarce can her infant tongue with easy voice
   Her name distinguish to another's ear;
   Yet had he lived, his power, and not my choice
   Had made me solemnly the contract swear.   20
   Have I not cause in such a change to joy?
   What though she be my niece, a princess born?
   Near blood's without respect, high birth a toy,
   Since love can teach us blood and kindred's scorn.
   What booted it that he did raise my head   25
   To be his realm's co-partner, kingdom's mate?
   Withal, he kept Graphina from my bed,
   More wished by me than thrice Judea's state.

---

1   Pheroras was engaged to one of Herod's young daughters.

Oh, could not he be skilful judge in love,
That doted so upon his Mariam's face?   30
He, for his passion, Doris did remove;
I needed not a lawful wife displace.
It could not be but he had power to judge!
But he that never grudged a kingdom's share,
This well-known happiness to me did grudge,   35
And meant to be therein without compare,
Else had I been his equal in love's host.
For though the diadem on Mariam's head
Corrupt the vulgar judgements, I will boast
Graphina's brow's as white, her cheeks as red.   40
Why speakst thou not fair creature? Move thy tongue,
For silence is a sign of discontent.
It were to both our loves too great a wrong
If now this hour do find thee sadly bent.

GRAPHINA.   Mistake me not my lord. Too oft have I   45
Desired this time to come with wingèd feet,
To be enwrapped with grief when 'tis too nigh.
You know my wishes ever yours did meet.
If I be silent, 'tis no more but fear
That I should say too little when I speak,   50
But since you will my imperfections bear,
In spite of doubt I will my silence break.
Yet might amazement tie my moving tongue,
But that I know before Pheroras' mind,
I have admirèd[1] your affection long,   55
And cannot yet therein a reason find.
Your hand hath lifted me from lowest state
To highest eminency, wondrous grace,
And me, your hand-maid, have you made your mate,
Though all but you alone do count me base.   60
You have preserved me pure at my request,
Though you so weak a vassal might constrain

---

1   Been amazed by, wondered at.

To yield to your high will. Then, last not best,
In my respect a princess you disdain.
Then need not all these favours study crave,   65
To be requited by a simple maid?
And study still, you know, must silence have:
Then be my cause for silence justly weighed.
But study cannot boot,[1] nor I requite,
Except your lowly hand-maid's steadfast love   70
And fast[2] obedience may your mind delight:
I will not promise more than I can prove.
PHERORAS. That study needs not. Let Graphina smile,
And I desire no greater recompense.
I cannot vaunt[3] me in a glorious style,   75
Nor show my love in far-fetched eloquence.
But this believe me: never Herod's heart
Hath held his prince-born beauty famèd wife
In nearer place than thou, fair virgin, art
To him that holds the glory of his life.   80
Should Herod's body leave the sepulcher
And entertain the severed ghost again,[4]
He should not be my nuptial hinderer,
Except he hindered it with dying pain.
Come fair Graphina, let us go in state,   85
This wish-endearèd time to celebrate.   *(Exeunt)*

Scene ii

(Enter Constabarus and Baba's sons)

BABA'S 1 SON. Now, valiant friend, you have our lives redeemed,
Which lives as saved by you, to you are due.

---

1 Would be of no use.
2 Fixed.
3 Glorify or praise.
4 Should Herod's body and soul be joined again in life.

Command and you shall see yourself esteemed;
Our lives and liberties belong to you.
This twice six years, with hazard of your life,   5
You have concealed us from the tyrant's sword;
Though cruel Herod's sister were your wife,
You durst in scorn of fear this grace afford.
In recompense we know not what to say;
A poor reward were thanks for such a merit.   10
Our truest friendship at your feet we lay,
The best requital to a noble spirit.
CONSTABARUS. Oh, how you wrong our friendship valiant youth!
With friends there is not such a word as debt,
Where amity is tied with bond of truth,   15
All benefits are there in common set.
Then is the Golden Age[1] with them renewed:
All names of properties are banished quite,
Division, and distinction are eschewed,
Each hath to what belongs to others, right.   20
And 'tis not, sure, so full a benefit,
Freely to give, as freely to require.
A bounteous act hath glory following it:
They cause the glory that the act desire.
All friendship should the pattern imitate   25
Of Jesse's son and valiant Jonathan,[2]
For neither sovereign's nor father's hate,
A friendship fixed on virtue sever can.
Too much of this; 'tis written in the heart,
And needs no amplifying with the tongue.   30
Now may you from your living tomb depart,
Where Herod's life hath kept you over long;
Too great an injury to a noble mind

---

1 In Classical mythology, an idealised, bygone era.
2 David and Jonathan: "the soule of Jonathan was knit with the soule of David,
   and Jonathan loved him, as his owne soule" (1 Samuel 18:1, *Geneva*). This
   friendship went against the express orders of Jonathan's father, King Saul.

To be quick buried.[1] You had purchased fame
Some years ago, but that you were confined,   35
While thousand meaner did advance their name.
Your best of life, the prime of all your years,
Your time of action, is from you bereft.
Twelve winters have you overpassed in fears,
Yet if you use it well, enough is left.   40
And who can doubt but you will use it well?
The sons of Baba have it by descent,
In all their thoughts each action to excel,
Boldly to act, and wisely to invent.
BABA'S 2 SON. Had it not like the hateful cuckoo been,[2]   45
Whose riper age his infant nurse doth kill,
So long we had not kept ourselves unseen,
But Constabarus' safety crossed our will.
For had the tyrant fixed his cruel eye
On our concealèd faces, wrath had swayed   50
His justice so, that he had forced us die.
And dearer price than life we should have paid,
For you, our truest friend, had fall'n with us,
And we, much like a house on pillars set,
Had clean depressed our prop. And therefore thus   55
Our ready will with our concealment met.
But now that you, fair lord, are dangerless,
The sons of Baba shall their rigour show,
And prove it was not baseness did oppress
Our hearts so long, but honour kept them low.   60
BABA'S 1 SON. Yet do I fear this tale of Herod's death
At last will prove a very tale indeed.
It gives me strongly in my mind, his breath
Will be preserved to make a number bleed.
I wish not therefore to be set at large   65
Yet peril to myself I do not fear.

---

1   Buried alive.
2   The cuckoo lays its egg in another bird's nest. As the young cuckoo grows, it
    ousts the resident birds.

Let us for some days longer be your charge,
Till we of Herod's state the truth do hear.
CONSTABARUS. What, art thou turned a coward noble youth,
That thou beginst to doubt, undoubted truth?   70
BABA'S 1 SON. Were it my brother's tongue that cast this doubt,
I from his heart would have the question out
With this keen fauchion![1] But 'tis you my lord
Against whose head I must not lift a sword,
I am so tied in gratitude.   75
CONSTABARUS.   Believe
You have no cause to take it ill.
If any word of mine your heart did grieve,
The word dissented from the speaker's will.
I know it was not fear the doubt begun,
But rather valour and your care of me: 80
A coward could not be your father's son.
Yet know I doubts unnecessary be,
For who can think that in Antonius' fall,
Herod, his bosom friend, should 'scape unbruised?
Then, Caesar, we might thee an idiot call,   85
If thou by him shouldst be so far abused.
BABA'S 2 SON. Lord Constabarus, let me tell you this:
Upon submission Caesar will forgive.
And therefore though the tyrant did amiss,
It may fall out that he will let him live.   90
Not many years ago it is since I,
Directed thither by my father's care,
In famous Rome for twice twelve months did live,
My life from Hebrew's cruelty to spare.
There, though I were but yet of boyish age,   95
I bent mine eye to mark, mine ears to hear,
Where I did see Octavius,[2] then a page,
When first he did to Julius'[3] sight appear.

---

1   Variant of falchion, a broad sword.
2   Octavius Caesar.
3   Julius Caesar.

Methought I saw such mildness in his face,
And such a sweetness in his looks did grow   100
Withal, commixed with so majestic grace,
His phys'nomy[1] his fortune did foreshow.
For this I am indebted to mine eye,
But then mine ear received more evidence.
By that I knew his love to clemency,   105
How he with hottest choler could dispense.

CONSTABARUS. But we have more than barely heard the news!
It hath been twice confirmed. And though some tongue
Might be so false, with false report t'abuse,
A false report hath never lasted long.   110
But be it so that Herod have his life,
Concealement would not then a whit avail,
For certain 'tis, that she that was my wife,
Would not to set her accusation fail.
And therefore now as good the venture give,   115
And free ourselves from blot of cowardice,
As show a pitiful desire to live,
For who can pity but they must despise?

BABA'S 1 SON. I yield, but to necessity I yield.
I dare upon this doubt[2] engage mine arm,   120
That Herod shall again this kingdom wield,
And prove his death to be a false alarm.

BABA'S 2 SON. I doubt[3] it too. God grant it be an error;
'Tis best without a cause to be in terror.
And rather had I, though my soul be mine,   125
My soul should lie, than prove a true divine.[4]

CONSTABARUS. Come, come, let fear go seek a dastard's[5] nest,
Undaunted courage lies in a noble breast.   *(Exeunt)*

---

1 Shortened form of physiognomy, meaning the face or countenance, when viewed
  as an index to the mind or character.
2 Suspicion.
3 Suspect.
4 One able to predict the future.
5 An ignoble coward.

Scene iii

(Enter Doris and Antipater)

DORIS. You royal buildings bow your lofty sides,
　　　And stoop to her that is by right your Queen;
　　　Let your humility upbraid the pride
　　　Of those in whom no due respect is seen.
　　　Nine times have we with trumpet's haughty sound,　　　5
　　　And banishing sour leaven from our taste,
　　　Observed the feast that takes the fruit from ground[1]
　　　Since I, fair city, did behold thee last.
　　　So long it is since Mariam's purer cheek
　　　Did rob from mine the glory. And so long　　　10
　　　Since I returned my native town to seek,
　　　And with me nothing but the sense of wrong,
　　　And thee, my boy, whose birth though great it were,
　　　Yet have thy after fortunes proved but poor.
　　　When thou wert born how little did I fear　　　15
　　　Thou shouldst be thrust from forth thy father's door.
　　　Art thou not Herod's right begotten son?
　　　Was not the hapless Doris Herod's wife?
　　　Yes, ere he had the Hebrew kingdom won,
　　　I was companion to his private life.　　　20
　　　Was I not fair enough to be a queen?
　　　Why, ere thou wert to me, false monarch, tied,
　　　My lake of beauty might as well be seen,
　　　As after I had lived five years thy bride.
　　　Yet then thine oaths came pouring like the rain,　　　25
　　　Which all affirmed my face without compare,
　　　And that if thou might'st Doris' love obtain,
　　　For all the world besides thou didst not care.

1　Doris is referring to annual Jewish festivals, such as the Passover and the offer-
　ing of the first fruits, to indicate that she has been banished from the city for
　nine years.

Then was I young, and rich, and nobly born,
And therefore worthy to be Herod's mate.   30
Yet thou, ungrateful, cast me off with scorn
When Heaven's purpose raised your meaner fate.
Oft have I begged for vengeance for this fact,
And with dejected knees, aspiring hands,
Have prayed the highest power to enact   35
The fall of her that on my trophy[1] stands.
Revenge I have according to my will,
Yet where I wished this vengeance did not light.
I wished it should high-hearted Mariam kill,
But it against my whilom[2] lord did fight.   40
With thee sweet boy I came, and came to try
If thou, before his bastards, might be placed
In Herod's royal seat and dignity.
But Mariam's infants here are only graced,
And now for us there doth no hope remain.   45
Yet we will not return till Herod's end
Be more confirmed. Perchance he is not slain;
So glorious fortunes may my boy attend.
For if he live, he'll think it doth suffice
That he to Doris shows such cruelty,   50
For as he did my wretched life despise,
So do I know I shall despisèd die.
Let him but prove as natural to thee,
As cruel to thy miserable mother.
His cruelty shall not upbraided be,   55
But in thy fortunes I his faults will smother.
ANTIPATER.   Each mouth within the city loudly cries
That Herod's death is certain. Therefore, we
Had best some subtle hidden plot devise,
That Mariam's children might subverted be   60
By poison's drink, or else by murderous knife;

---

1   A structure erected on a battlefield or other public place, dedicated to a divinity
    and hung with riches or spoils.
2   Previous.

So we may be advanced, it skills[1] not how.
They are but bastards, you were Herod's wife,
And foul adultery blotteth Mariam's brow.

DORIS.   They are too strong to be by us removed,   65
Or else revenge's foulest spotted face
By our detested wrongs might be approved.[2]
But weakness must to greater power give place.
But let us now retire to grieve alone,
For solitariness best fitteth moan.   *(Exeunt)* 70

Scene iv

(Enter Silleus and Constabarus, meeting)

SILLEUS.   Well met Judean lord, the only wight[3]
Silleus wished to see. I am to call
Thy tongue to strict account.
CONSTABARUS.   For what despite?
I ready am to hear, and answer all.
But if directly at the cause I guess   5
That breeds this challenge, you must pardon me,
And now some other ground of fight profess,
For I have vowed, vows must unbroken be.
SILLEUS.   What may be your exception? Let me know.
CONSTABARUS.   Why, aught concerning Salome. My sword   10
Shall not be wielded for a cause so low;
A blow for her my arm will scorn t'afford.
SILLEUS.   It is for slandering her unspotted name.
And I will make thee in thy vow's despite,

---

1   The *OED* lists several meanings, but the rare meaning of "to care" seems to be
    appropriate here, to give the reading "It does not matter how."
2   The modern meaning applies although the sense is confused by the imagery. The
    act of revenge, personified as "revenge's foulest face" would be approved by Doris
    and Antipater's similarly personified "detested wrongs," if Mariam and her family
    were not so powerful.
3   Living creature.

Suck up the breath that did my mistress blame,   15
And swallow it again to do her right.
CONSTABARUS.   I prithee give some other quarrel ground.
  To find beginning, rail against my name,
  Or strike me first, or let some scarlet wound
  Inflame my courage. Give me words of shame;   20
  Do thou our Moses' sacred laws disgrace;
  Deprave our nation, do me some despite;
  I'm apt enough to fight in any case,
  But yet for Salome I will not fight.
SILLEUS.   Nor I for aught but Salome. My sword,   25
  That owes his service to her sacred name,
  Will not an edge for other cause afford;
  In other fight I am not sure of fame.
CONSTABARUS.   For her, I pity thee enough already.
  For her, I therefore will not mangle[1] thee.   30
  A woman with a heart so most unsteady,
  Will of herself sufficient torture be.
  I cannot envy for so light a gain.
  Her mind with such unconstancy doth run,
  As with a word thou didst her love obtain,   35
  So with a word she will from thee be won.
  So light, as her possession's for most, day
  Is her affections lost. To me 'tis known.[2]
  As good go hold the wind as make her stay.
  She never loves, but till she call her own.   40
  She merely is a painted sepulchre,[3]
  That is both fair and vilely foul at once:
  Though on her outside graces garnish her,
  Her mind is filled with worse than rotten bones,

---

1   Mutilate.
2   The denigrating tone and general sense of these two lines is clear, although they
    have been difficult to punctuate effectively. The punctuation used here attempts to
    convey the meaning "A woman as inconstant as she, whom most men can possess,
    changes her affections daily, I know."
3   A tomb.

And ever ready lifted is her hand, 45
To aim destruction at a husband's throat.
For proofs, Josephus and myself do stand,
Though once on both of us she seemed to dote.
Her mouth, though serpent-like, it never hisses,
Yet like a serpent, poisons where it kisses. 50

SILLEUS. Well, Hebrew, well! Thou bark'st, but wilt not bite.

CONSTABARUS. I tell thee still, for her I will not fight.

SILLEUS. Why then I call thee coward.

CONSTABARUS.   From my heart
I give thee thanks. A coward's hateful name
Cannot to valiant minds a blot impart 55
And therefore I with joy receive the same.
Thou know'st I am no coward. Thou wert by
At the Arabian battle th'other day,
And saw'st my sword with daring valiancy
Amongst the faint Arabians cut my way. 60
The blood of foes no more could let it shine,
And 'twas enamellèd with some of thine.
But now have at thee! Not for Salome
I fight, but to discharge a coward's style.
Here 'gins the fight that shall not parted be, 65
Before a soul or two endure exile!   *(They fight)*

SILLEUS. Thy sword hath made some windows for my blood,
To show a horrid crimson phys'nomy.
To breathe for both of us methinks 'twere good,
The day will give us time enough to die. 70

CONSTABARUS. With all my heart take breath. Thou shalt have time,
And if thou list a twelvemonth. Let us end.
Into thy cheeks there doth a paleness climb;
Thou canst not from my sword thyself defend.
What needest thou for Salome to fight? 75
Thou hast her, and may'st keep her, none strives for her.
I willingly to thee resign my right,
For in my very soul I do abhor her.
Thou seest that I am fresh, unwounded yet,

Then not for fear I do this offer make.   80
Thou art, with loss of blood, to fight unfit,
For here is one, and there another take.

SILLEUS.   I will not leave, as long as breath remains
Within my wounded body. Spare your words.
My heart in blood's stead, courage entertains;   85
Salome's love no place for fear affords.

CONSTABARUS.   Oh could thy soul but prophesy like mine,
I would not wonder thou shouldst long to die.
For Salome, if I aright divine,
Will be than death a greater misery.   90

SILLEUS.   Then list, I'll breathe no longer.

CONSTABARUS.   Do thy will.
I hateless fight, and charitably kill.   *(They fight)*
Pity thyself Silleus. Let not death
Intrude before his time into thy heart!
Alas it is too late to fear! His breath   95
Is from his body now about to part.
How far'st thou brave Arabian?

SILLEUS.   Very well.
My leg is hurt, I can no longer fight.
It only grieves me that so soon I fell,
Before fair Salom's wrongs I came to right.   100

CONSTABARUS.   Thy wounds are less than mortal. Never fear,
Thou shalt a safe and quick recovery find.
Come, I will thee unto my lodging bear,
I hate thy body, but I love thy mind.

SILLEUS.   Thanks noble Jew, I see a courteous foe.   105
Stern enmity to friendship can no art.[1]
Had not my heart and tongue engaged me so,
I would from thee no foe, but f[Male friendship
My heart to Salome is tied too f[ast]
To leave her love for friendship,   110

---

1   "No art can transform stern enmity to friendship."

Shall be employed to make your favour last,
And I will honour Constabarus still.
CONSTABARUS. I ope my bosom to thee, and will take
    Thee in, as friend, and grieve for thy complaint.
    But if we do not expedition make,   115
    Thy loss of blood I fear will make thee faint.   *(Exeunt)*

CHORUS.

To hear a tale with ears prejudicate,
It spoils the judgement, and corrupts the sense,
That human error giv'n to every state,
Is greater enemy to innocence.
    It makes us foolish, heady, rash, unjust;   5
    It makes us never try before we trust.[1]

It will confound the meaning, change the words,
For it our sense of hearing much deceives.
Besides, no time to judgement it affords,
To weigh the circumstance our ear receives.   10
    The ground of accidents it never tries,
    But makes us take for truth ten thousand lies.

Our ears and hearts are apt to hold for good,
That we ourselves do most desire to be,
And then we drown objections in the flood   15
Of partiality. 'Tis that we see
    That makes false rumours long with credit past,
    Though they like rumours must conclude at last.

The greatest part of us prejudicate,
With wishing Herod's death do hold it true.   20
The being once deluded doth not bate[2]
The credit to a better likelihood due.

---

1 Cf. Nuntio's words in V.i.
2 Lessen.

Those few that wish it not, the multitude
Do carry headlong, so they doubts conclude.

They[1] not object the weak uncertain ground,   25
Whereon they[2] built this tale of Herod's end,
Whereof the author scarcely can be found,
And all because their wishes that way bend.
    They think not of the peril that ensu'th,
    If this should prove contrary to the truth.   30

On this same doubt, on this so light a breath,
They pawn their lives and fortunes. For they all
Behave them as the news of Herod's death
They did of most undoubted credit call.
    But if their actions now do rightly hit,   35
    Let them commend their fortune, not their wit.

---

1   The minority who doubted the rumour.
2   The majority who perpetuate the rumour.

ACT III

Scene i

(Enter Pheroras and Salome)

PHERORAS. Urge me no more Graphina to forsake,
    Not twelve hours since I married her for love.
    And do you think a sister's power can make
    A resolute decree so soon remove?
SALOME. Poor minds they are that honour not affects.   5
PHERORAS. Who hunts for honour, happiness neglects.
SALOME. You might have been both of felicity
    And honour too, in equal measure seized.
PHERORAS. It is not you can tell so well as I
    What 'tis can make me happy, or displeased.   10
SALOME. To match, for neither beauty nor respects,
    One mean of birth, but yet of meaner mind,
    A woman full of natural defects,
    I wonder what your eye in her could find.
PHERORAS. Mine eye found loveliness, mine ear found wit,   15
    To please the one, and to enchant the other.
    Grace on her eye, mirth on her tongue doth sit,
    In looks a child, in wisdom's house a mother.
SALOME. But say you thought her fair, as none thinks else,
    Knows not Pheroras beauty is a blast?[1]   20
    Much like this flower which today excels,
    But longer than a day it will not last.
PHERORAS. Her wit exceeds her beauty.
SALOME.   Wit may show
    The way to ill, as well as good you know.

---

1   Something transient. However, the *OED* gives an alternative meaning, which
    could also be implied in this context: "To bring infamy upon; to discredit effec-
    tually, ruin, destroy." Salome later makes use of Mariam's beauty as a means to
    ruin her.

PHERORAS. But wisdom is the porter[1] of her head,   25
    And bars all wicked words from issuing thence.
SALOME. But of a porter, better were you sped,[2]
    If she against their entrance made defence.
PHERORAS. But wherefore comes the sacred Ananell,
    That hitherward his hasty steps doth bend?   30
    Great sacrifcer y'are arrivèd well,
    Ill news from holy mouth I not attend.[3]

Scene ii

(Enter Ananell)

ANANELL. My lips, my son, with peaceful tidings blessed,
    Shall utter honey to your list'ning ear.
    A word of death comes not from priestly breast,
    I speak of life: in life there is no fear.
    And for the news I did the Heavens salute,   5
    And filled the temple with my thankful voice,
    For though that mourning may not me pollute,
    At pleasing accidents I may rejoice.
PHERORAS. Is Herod then revived from certain death?
SALOME. What, can your news restore my brother's breath?   10
ANANELL. Both so, and so: the King is safe and sound,
    And did such grace in royal Caesar meet,
    That he with larger style than ever crowned,
    Within this hour Jerusalem will greet.
    I did but come to tell you, and must back   15
    To make preparitives for sacrifice.
    I knew his death your hearts, like mine, did rack,
    Though to conceal it, proved you wise.   *(Exit)*

---

1 Gatekeeper, doorkeeper.
2 Discharged, in the sense that such a porter (i.e., wisdom) would better discharge
    his duties if he kept Graphina chaste.
3 Expect.

SALOME. How can my joy sufficiently appear?
PHERORAS. A heavier tale did never pierce mine ear.   20
SALOME. Now Salome of happiness may boast.
PHERORAS. But now Pheroras is in danger most.
SALOME. I shall enjoy the comfort of my life.
PHERORAS. And I shall lose it, losing of my wife.
SALOME. Joy heart, for Constabarus shall be slain!   25
PHERORAS. Grieve soul, Graphina shall from me be ta'en!
SALOME. Smile cheeks, the fair Silleus shall be mine.
PHERORAS. Weep eyes, for I must with a child combine.[1]
SALOME. Well brother, cease your moans. On one condition
    I'll undertake to win the King's consent,   30
    Graphina still shall be in your tuition,[2]
    And her with you be ne'er the less content.
PHERORAS. What's the condition? Let me quickly know,
    That I as quickly your command may act,
    Were it to see what herbs in Ophir[3] grow,   35
    Or that the lofty Tyrus[4] might be sacked.
SALOME. 'Tis not so hard a task. It is no more
    But tell the King that Constabarus hid
    The sons of Baba, doomed to death before;
    And 'tis no more than Constabarus did.   40
    And tell him more, that I for Herod's sake,
    Not able to endure our brother's foe,
    Did with a bill our separation make,
    Though loth from Constabarus else to go.
PHERORAS. Believe this tale for told. I'll go from hence,   45
    In Herod's ear the Hebrew to deface.

---

1   Marry.
2   Protection, care.
3   A legendary place, probably situated in Arabia, where fine gold, perfume and
    precious stones were to be found. See 1 Kings 9:28 and 10:11, *Geneva*.
4   Tyre. A city, famous in the Ancient World for its silk, glass and purple dye industry.
    In 63 BC, Tyre came under the rule of Mark Antony, who demanded the return
    of Jewish property taken by the Tyrians and forbade any damage to be done to
    the city.

And I that never studied eloquence,
Do mean with eloquence this tale to grace.   (Exit)
SALOME.   This will be Constabarus' quick dispatch,
          Which from my mouth would lesser credit find.   50
          Yet shall he not decease without a match,
          For Mariam shall not linger long behind.
          First jealousy, if that avail not, fear
          Shall be my minister to work her end.
          A common error moves not Herod's ear,   55
          Which doth so firmly to his Mariam bend.
          She shall be chargèd with so horrid crime,
          As Herod's fear shall turn his love to hate.
          I'll make some swear that she desires to climb,
          And seeks to poison him for his estate.   60
          I scorn that she should live my birth t'upbraid,
          To call me base and hungry Edomite.
          With patient show her choler I betrayed,[1]
          And watched the time to be revenged by slight.
          Now tongue of mine with scandal load her name,   65
          Turn hers to fountains, Herod's eyes to flame.
          Yet first I will begin Pheroras' suit,
          That he my earnest business may effect;
          And I of Mariam will keep me mute,
          Till first some other doth her name detect.[2]   70
                                        (Enter Silleus' man)
          Who's there? Silleus' man? How fares your lord,
          That your aspects do bear the badge of sorrow?
SILLEUS' MAN.   He hath the marks of Constabarus' sword,
          And for a while desires your sight to borrow.
SALOME.   My heavy curse the hateful sword pursue,   75
          My heavier curse on the more hateful arm
          That wounded my Silleus. But renew
          Your tale again. Hath he no mortal harm?

---

1   Salome's patient endurance made Mariam's temper appear in the worst possible light.
2   Expose to scandal.

SILLEUS' MAN.   No sign of danger doth in him appear,
     Nor are his wounds in place of peril seen.   80
     He bids you be assured you need not fear;
     He hopes to make you yet Arabia's Queen.
SALOME.   Commend my heart to be Silleus' charge.
     Tell him, my brother's sudden coming now
     Will give my foot no room to walk at large.   85
     But I will see him yet ere night, I vow.   *(Exeunt)*

Scene iii

(Enter Mariam and Sohemus)

MARIAM.   Sohemus, tell me what the news may be
     That makes your eyes so full, your cheeks so blue?
SOHEMUS.   I know not how to call them. Ill for me
     'Tis sure they are: not so I hope for you.
     Herod –
MARIAM.   Oh, what of Herod?
SOHEMUS.   Herod lives.   5
MARIAM.   How! Lives? What, in some cave or forest hid?
SOHEMUS.   Nay, back returned with honour. Caesar gives
     Him greater grace than e'er Antonius did.
MARIAM.   Foretell the ruin of my family,
     Tell me that I shall see our city burned,   10
     Tell me I shall a death disgraceful die,
     But tell me not that Herod is returned.
SOHEMUS.   Be not impatient madam, be but mild,
     His love to you again will soon be bred.
MARIAM.   I will not to his love be reconciled,   15
     With solemn vows I have forsworn his bed.
SOHEMUS.   But you must break those vows.
MARIAM.   I'll rather break
     The heart of Mariam. Cursèd is my fate –

But speak no more to me, in vain ye speak –
To live with him I so profoundly hate! 20
SOHEMUS. Great Queen, you must to me your pardon give,
Sohemus cannot now your will obey.
If your command should me to silence drive,
It were not to obey but to betray.
Reject, and slight my speeches, mock my faith, 25
Scorn my observance, call my counsel nought.
Though you regard not what Sohemus saith,
Yet will I ever freely speak my thought.
I fear ere long I shall fair Mariam see
In woeful state, and by herself undone. 30
Yet for your issue's sake more temp'rate be,
The heart by affability is won.
MARIAM. And must I to my prison turn again?
Oh, now I see I was an hypocrite!
I did this morning for his death complain, 35
And yet do mourn, because he lives ere night.
When I his death believed, compassion wrought,
And was the stickler[1] 'twixt my heart and him.
But now that curtain's drawn from off my thought,
Hate doth appear again with visage grim 40
And paints the face of Herod in my heart,
In horrid colours with detested look.
Then fear would come, but scorn doth play her part,
And saith that scorn with fear can never brook.
I know I could enchain him with a smile 45
And lead him captive with a gentle word.
I scorn my look should ever man beguile,
Or other speech, than meaning to afford.[2]
Else Salome in vain might spend her wind,
In vain might Herod's mother whet her tongue, 50
In vain had they complotted and combined,

---

1 A mediator between combatants or disputants.
2 "I will not say anything that I do not mean."

For I could overthrow them all ere long.
Oh what a shelter is mine innocence,
To shield me from the pangs of inward grief.
'Gainst all mishaps it is my fair defence,   55
And to my sorrows yields a large relief.
To be commandress of the triple earth,
And sit in safety from a fall secure,
To have all nations celebrate my birth,
I would not that my spirit were impure.   60
Let my distressèd state unpitied be,
Mine innocence is hope enough for me.   *(Exit)*
SOHEMUS.   Poor guiltless Queen! Oh that my wish might place
A little temper[1] now about thy heart!
Unbridled speech is Mariam's worst disgrace,   65
And will endanger her without desert.
I am in greater hazard. O'er my head
The fatal axe doth hang unsteadily.
My disobedience once discoverèd,
Will shake it down. Sohemus so shall die.   70
For when the King shall find we thought his death
Had been as certain as we see his life,
And marks withal I slighted so his breath,
As to preserve alive his matchless wife –
Nay more, to give to Alexandra's hand   75
The regal dignity, the sovereign power,
How I had yielded up at her command,
The strength of all the city, David's tower –
What more than common death may I expect,
Since I too well do know his cruelty?   80
'Twere death a word of Herod's to neglect,
What then to do directly contrary?
Yet, life, I quit thee with a willing spirit,
And think thou couldst not better be employed.
I forfeit thee for her that more doth merit,   85

---

1   Moderation.

Ten such were better dead than she destroyed.
But fare thee well chaste Queen. Well may I see
The darkness palpable,[1] and rivers part
The sun stand still, nay more, retorted[2] be,
But never woman with so pure a heart.   90
Thine eyes' grave majesty keeps all in awe,
And cuts the wings of every loose desire.
Thy brow is table to the modest law,
Yet though we dare not love, we may admire.
And if I die, it shall my soul content,   95
My breath in Mariam's service shall be spent.   (*Exit*)

CHORUS.

'Tis not enough for one that is a wife
To keep her spotless from an act of ill,
But from suspicion she should free her life,
And bare herself of power as well as will.
   'Tis not so glorious for her to be free,   5
   As by her proper self restrained to be.

When she hath spacious ground to walk upon,
Why on the ridge should she desire to go?
It is no glory to forbear alone
Those things that may her honour overthrow.   10
   But 'tis thank-worthy, if she will not take
   All lawful liberties for honour's sake.

That wife her hand against her fame doth rear,
That more than to her lord alone will give
A private word to any second ear.   15
And though she may with reputation live,
   Yet though most chaste, she doth her glory blot,
   And wounds her honour, though she kills it not.

---

1 Tangible.
2 Repulsed or driven back.

When to their husbands they themselves do bind,
Do they not wholly give themselves away? 20
Or give they but their body not their mind,
Reserving that, though best, for others, pray?
    No sure, their thoughts no more can be their own,
    And therefore should to none but one be known.

Then she usurps upon another's right, 25
That seeks to be by public language graced;
And though her thoughts reflect with purest light,
Her mind if not peculiar[1] is not chaste.
    For in a wife it is no worse to find,
    A common body, than a common mind. 30

And every mind though free from thought of ill,
That out of glory seeks a worth to show,
When any's ears but one therewith they fill,
Doth in a sort her pureness overthrow.
    Now Mariam had, but that to this she bent, 35
    Been free from fear, as well as innocent.[2]

---

1   Particular to one person only.
2   "If Mariam had followed this principle, her state of innocence would never have
been called into question and so she would have been free from the fear of con-
demnation."

ACT IV

Scene i

(Enter Herod and his attendants)

HEROD.   Hail happy city! Happy in thy store,[1]
    And happy that thy buildings such we see;
    More happy in the temple where w'adore,
    But most of all that Mariam lives in thee. *(Enter Nuntio)*
    Art thou returned? How fares my Mariam?   5
NUNTIO.   She's well my lord, and will anon be here
    As you commanded.
HEROD.   Muffle up thy brow,
    Thou day's dark taper![2] Mariam will appear,
    And where she shines, we need not thy dim light.
    Oh haste thy steps rare creature, speed thy pace,   10
    And let thy presence make the day more bright,
    And cheer the heart of Herod with thy face.
    It is an age since I from Mariam went,
    Methinks our parting was in David's days,[3]
    The hours are so increased by discontent.   15
    Deep sorrow, Joshua-like[4] the season stays
    But when I am with Mariam, time runs on:
    Her sight can make months minutes, days of weeks.
    An hour is then no sooner come than gone,
    When in her face mine eye for wonders seeks.   20
    You world commanding city, Europe's grace,[5]
    Twice hath my curious eye your streets surveyed,
    And I have seen the statue-fillèd place,

---

1   Treasure.
2   Candle. Herod is referring to the sun, whose light, he says, is rendered unneccessary
     because of the light produced by Mariam's beauty.
3   According to Josephus, David ruled between 1073 and 1034 BC (*Ant.*, 159-85 and 399).
4   At Joshua's request, God made the sun and moon stand still, until the Israelites
     had conquered their enemies, the Amorites (Joshua 10:12-14, *Geneva*).
5   Rome.

That once if not for grief had been betrayed.
I, all you Roman beauties have beheld,   25
And seen the shows your Ediles[1] did prepare;
I saw the sum of what in you excelled,
Yet saw no miracle like Mariam rare.
The fair and famous Livia,[2] Caesar's love,
The world's commanding mistress, did I see,   30
Whose beauties both the world and Rome approve,
Yet, Mariam, Livia is not like to thee.
Be patient but a little while, mine eyes,
Within your compassed[3] limits be contained;
That object straight shall your desires suffice,   35
From which you were so long a while restrained.
How wisely Mariam doth the time delay,
Lest sudden joy my sense should suffocate.
I am prepared, thou needst no longer stay.   *(Exit Nuntio)*
Who's there? My Mariam, more than happy fate?   40
Oh no, it is Pheroras. Welcome brother!
Now for a while, I must my passion smother.

Scene ii

(Enter Pheroras)

PHERORAS.   All health and safety wait upon my lord,
   And may you long in prosperous fortunes live,
   With Rome-commanding Caesar at accord,
   And have all honours that the world can give.
HEROD.   Oh brother, now thou speakst not from thy heart!   5
   No, thou hast struck a blow at Herod's love

---

1   The Aediles were two subordinate officials of the plebs, who probably superin-
    tended the common temple (aedes) and the cult of the plebs, that of Ceres. They
    also took responsibility for urban adminstration and the public games.
2   Livia Drusilla, (55 BC-AD 29), wife of Octavius (Augustus) Caesar.
3   Bounded.

That cannot quickly from my memory part,
Though Salome did me to pardon move.
Valiant Phasaelus,[1] now to thee farewell,
Thou wert my kind and honourable brother   10
Oh hapless hour, when you self-stricken fell,
Thou father's image, glory of thy mother
Had I desired a greater suit of thee,
Than to withhold thee from a harlot's bed,
Thou wouldst have granted it. But now I see   15
All are not like that in a womb are bred.
Thou wouldst not, hadst thou heard of Herod's death,
Have made his burial time thy bridal hour;
Thou wouldst with clamours, not with joyful breath,
Have showed the news to be not sweet but sour.   20

PHERORAS. Phasaelus great worth I know did stain
Pheroras' petty valour,[2] but they lie
(Excepting you yourself) that dare maintain
That he did honour Herod more than I.
For what I showed, love's power constrained me show,   25
And pardon loving faults for Mariam's sake.

HEROD. Mariam, where is she?

PHERORAS.   Nay, I do not know,
But absent use of her fair name I make.
You have forgiven greater faults than this.
For Constabarus, that against your will   30
Preserved the sons of Baba, lives in bliss,
Though you commanded him the youths to kill.

HEROD. Go, take a present order for his death,
And let those traitors feel the worst of fears!
Now Salome will whine to beg his breath,   35
But I'll be deaf to prayers and blind to tears.

PHERORAS. He is, my lord, from Salome divorced,
Though her affection did to leave him grieve,

---

1 Herod's brother, who killed himself when taken as a prisoner of war (*Ant.*, 373).
2 "Phasaelus great valour made mine seem worthless."

Yet was she by her love to you enforced
To leave the man that would your foes relieve. 40
HEROD. Then haste them to their death. I will requite

Thee gentle Mariam – Salome I mean.
The thought of Mariam doth so steal my spirit,
My mouth from speech of her I cannot wean.

Scene iii

(Enter Mariam)

HEROD. And here she comes indeed! Happily met,
My best and dearest half. What ails my dear?
Thou dost the difference certainly forget
'Twixt dusky habits and a time so clear.
MARIAM. My lord, I suit my garment to my mind, 5
And there no cheerful colours can I find.
HEROD. Is this my welcome? Have I longed so much
To see my dearest Mariam discontent?
What is't that is the cause thy heart to touch?
Oh speak, that I thy sorrow may prevent. 10
Art thou not Jewry's Queen, and Herod's too?
Be my commandress, be my sovereign guide;
To be by thee directed I will woo,
For in thy pleasure lies my highest pride.
Or if thou think Judea's narrow bound 15
Too strict a limit for thy great command,
Thou shalt be Empress of Arabia crowned,
For thou shalt rule, and I will win the land.
I'll rob the holy David's sepulchre
To give thee wealth, if thou for wealth do care. 20
Thou shalt have all they did with him inter,
And I for thee will make the temple bare.

MARIAM. I neither have of power nor riches want,
  I have enough, nor do I wish for more.
  Your offers to my heart no ease can grant   25
  Except they could my brother's life restore.
  No, had you wished the wretched Mariam glad,
  Or had your love to her been truly tied,
  Nay, had you not desired to make her sad,
  My brother nor my grandsire had not died.   30
HEROD. Wilt thou believe no oaths to clear thy lord?
  How oft have I with execration[1] sworn?
  Thou art by me beloved, by me adored,
  Yet are my protestations heard with scorn.
  Hircanus plotted to deprive my head   35
  Of this long settlèd honour that I wear,
  And therefore I did justly doom him dead,
  To rid the realm from peril, me from fear.[2]
  Yet I for Mariam's sake do so repent
  The death of one whose blood she did inherit,   40
  I wish I had a kingdom's treasure spent,
  So I had ne'er expelled Hircanus' spirit.
  As I affected that same noble youth,
  In lasting infamy my name enrol
  If I not mourned his death with hearty truth.   45
  Did I not show to him my earnest love
  When I to him the priesthood did restore?
  And did for him a living priest remove
  Which never had been done but once before.[3]
MARIAM. I know that moved by importunity[4]   50
  You made him priest, and shortly after die.

---

1 Driving out with a curse.
2 According to Josephus, this version of events is found in Herod's memoirs. Josephus also
  relates the version which suggests that Hircanus' treason was a fabrication (*Ant.*, 394).
3 A high priest had been removed from office twice before, according to Josephus
  (*Ant.*, 384).
4 "Troublesome pertinacity in solicitation." (*OED*) This evokes Josephus' description
  of Mariam and Alexandra's request that Aristobolus be promoted to high priest
  (*Ant.*, 385).

HEROD. I will not speak, unless to be believed!
　　This froward[1] humour will not do you good.
　　It hath too much already Herod grieved
　　To think that you on terms of hate have stood.　　　　55
　　Yet smile my dearest Mariam, do but smile,
　　And I will all unkind conceits exile.
MARIAM. I cannot frame disguise, nor never taught
　　My face a look dissenting from my thought.
HEROD. By Heav'n you vex me, build not on my love!　　60
MARIAM. I will not build on so unstable ground.
HEROD. Nought is so fixed, but peevishness may move.
MARIAM. 'Tis better slightest cause than none were found.
HEROD. Be judge yourself, if ever Herod sought
　　Or would be moved a cause of change to find.　　　　65
　　Yet let your look declare a milder thought,
　　My heart again you shall to Mariam bind.
　　How oft did I for you my mother chide,
　　Revile my sister, and my brother rate,[2]
　　And tell them all my Mariam they belied?　　　　　　70
　　Distrust me still, if these be signs of hate.

Scene iv

(Enter Butler)

HEROD. What hast thou here?
BUTLER.　　　　　　　　　　　　A drink procuring love.
　　The Queen desired me to deliver it.
MARIAM. Did I? Some hateful practice this will prove!
　　Yet can it be no worse than Heavens permit.
HEROD. Confess the truth, thou wicked instrument　　　5
　　To her outrageous will! 'Tis poison sure!

1　Peevish, perverse of humour.
2　Scold, chide, berate.

Tell true, and thou shalt 'scape the punishment,
Which if thou do conceal, thou shalt endure.
BUTLER. I know not, but I doubt it be no less,
Long since the hate of you her heart did seize. 10
HEROD. Know'st thou the cause thereof?
BUTLER. My lord, I guess
Sohemus told the tale that did displease.
HEROD. Oh Heaven! Sohemus false? Go let him die –
Stay not to suffer him to speak a word. *(Exit Butler)*
Oh damnèd villain, did he falsify 15
The oath he swore ev'n of his own accord?
Now do I know thy falsehood, painted devil,
Thou white enchantress. Oh thou art so foul,
That Hyssop[1] cannot cleanse thee, worst of evil.
A beauteous body hides a loathsome soul. 20
Your love, Sohemus, moved by his affection,
Though he have ever heretofore been true,
Did blab, forsooth, that I did give direction,
If we were put to death to slaughter you.
And you in black revenge attended[2] now 25
To add a murder to your breach of vow.
MARIAM. Is this a dream?
HEROD. Oh Heaven, that 'twere no more!
I'll give my realm to who can prove it so!
I would I were like any beggar poor,
So I for false my Mariam did not know; 30
Foul pith contained in the fairest rind,
That ever graced a cedar.[3] Oh thine eye
Is pure as heaven, but impure thy mind,
And for impurity shall Mariam die.
Why didst thou love Sohemus? 35

---

1 A plant of which the twigs were used for sprinkling in Jewish rites; a bunch of
   this was used in ceremonial purification.
2 Waited with intent.
3 A fragrant wood, used for the construction of palaces and significant buildings and
   hence very important in the Jewish economy at the time of the play's events.

MARIAM.   They can tell
That say I loved him, Mariam says not so.
HEROD.   Oh cannot impudence the coals expel,
    That for thy love in Herod's bosom glow?
    It is as plain as water, and denial
    Makes of thy falsehood but a greater trial.   40
    Hast thou beheld thyself, and couldst thou stain
    So rare perfection? Even for love of thee
    I do profoundly hate thee. Wert thou plain,[1]
    Thou shouldst the wonder of Judea be.
    But oh, thou art not. Hell itself lies hid   45
    Beneath thy heavenly show. Yet never wert thou chaste.
    Thou mightst exalt, pull down, command, forbid,
    And be above the wheel of fortune placed.[2]
    Hadst thou complotted Herod's massacre,
    That so thy son a monarch might be styled,   50
    Not half so grievous such an action were,
    As once to think that Mariam is defiled.
    Bright workmanship of nature-sullied ore,
    With pitchèd darkness now thine end shall be.
    Thou shalt not live, fair fiend, to cozen[3] more,   55
    With heav'nly semblance, as thou coz'nedst me.
    Yet must I love thee in despite of death,
    And thou shalt die in the despite of love,
    For neither shall my love prolong thy breath,
    Nor shall thy loss of breath my love remove.   60
    I might have seen thy falsehood in thy face –
    Where couldst thou get thy stars that served for eyes
    Except by theft? And theft is foul disgrace.
    This had appeared before, were Herod wise.
    But I'm a sot, a very sot, no better;   65
    My wisdom long ago a-wand'ring fell.
    Thy face encount'ring it, my wit did fetter,

---

1   Free from duplicity, honest.
2   Beyond the reach of the vagaries of fortune.
3   Trick, dupe.

And made me for delight my freedom sell.
Give me my heart false creature! 'Tis a wrong
My guiltless heart should now with thine be slain.   70
Thou hadst no right to lock it up so long,
And with usurper's name I Mariam stain.   *(Enter Butler)*

HEROD. Have you designed Sohemus to his end?

BUTLER. I have my lord.

HEROD.   Then call our royal guard
To do as much for Mariam. They offend   *(Exit Butler)* 75
Leave ill unblamed, or good without reward. *(Enter Soldiers)*
Here take her to her death. Come back! Come back!
What? Meant I to deprive the world of light,
To muffle Jewry in the foulest black,
That ever was an opposite to white?   80
Why whither would you carry her?

SOLDIERS.   You bade
We should conduct her to her death, my lord.

HEROD. Why, sure I did not? Herod was not mad.
Why should she feel the fury of the sword?
Oh now the grief returns into my heart,   85
And pulls me piecemeal! Love and hate do fight:
And now hath love acquired the greater part,
Yet now hath hate affection conquered quite.
And therefore bear her hence! And, Hebrew, why
Seize you with lion's paws the fairest lamb   90
Of all the flock? She must not, shall not, die!
Without her I most miserable am;
And with her more than most! Away, away!
But bear her but to prison not to death.
          (Exeunt Soldiers with Mariam)
And is she gone indeed – stay, villains, stay!   95
Her looks alone preserved your sovereign's breath.
Well let her go, but yet she shall not die.
I cannot think she meant to poison me,
But certain 'tis she lived too wantonly,
And therefore shall she never more be free.   *(Exit)* 100

Scene v

(Enter Butler)

BUTLER. Foul villain, can thy pitchy-coloured[1] soul
Permit thine ear to hear her causeless doom,
And not enforce thy tongue that tale control
That must unjustly bring her to her tomb?
Oh Salome thou hast thyself repaid,   5
For all the benefits that thou hast done.
Thou art the cause I have the Queen betrayed,
Thou hast my heart to darkest falsehood won.
I am condemned. Heav'n gave me not my tongue
To slander innocents, to lie, deceive,   10
To be the hateful instrument to wrong,
The earth of greatest glory to bereave.
My sin ascends and doth to heaven cry:
"It is the blackest deed that ever was!"
And there doth sit an angel notary   15
That doth record it down in leaves of brass.
Oh how my heart doth quake! Achitophel,[2]
Thou foundst a means thyself from shame to free,
And sure my soul approves thou didst not well;
All follow some, and I will follow thee.   *(Exit)* 20

---

1 Black.
2 Achitophel joined forces with Absalom against his father, David. When Absalom
   rejected Achitophel's counsels, Achitophel "saddled his asse, and arose, and went
   home unto his citie and put his household in ordre, and hanged himself and
   dyed" (2 Samuel 17:23, *Geneva*).

Scene vi

(Enter Constabarus, Baba's sons and their guard)

CONSTABARUS. Now here we step our last, the way to death,
We must not tread this way a second time.
Yet let us resolutely yield our breath,
Death is the only ladder, heav'n to climb.
BABA'S 1 SON. With willing mind I could myself resign,   5
But yet it grieves me, with a grief untold,
Our death should be accompanied with thine,
Our friendship we to thee have dearly sold.
CONSTABARUS. Still wilt thou wrong the sacred name of friend?
Then shouldst thou never style it friendship more,   10
But base mechanic traffic,[1] that doth lend,
Yet will be sure they shall the debt restore.
I could with needless compliment return,
This for thy ceremony I could say:
"'Tis I that made the fire your house to burn,   15
For but for me she would not you betray."
Had not the damnèd woman sought mine end,
You had not been the subject of her hate.
You never did her hateful mind offend,
Nor could your deaths have freed our nuptial fate.   20
Therefore fair friends, though you were still unborn,
Some other subtlety devised should be,
Whereby my life, though guiltless, should be torn.
Thus have I proved, 'tis you that die for me,
And therefore should I weakly now lament.   25
You have but done your duties. Friends should die
Alone, their friends' disaster to prevent,
Though not compelled by strong necessity.
But now farewell, fair city. Never more
Shall I behold your beauty shining bright!   30

---

1   The lowest form of commercial transaction.

Farewell of Jewish men the worthy store,
But no farewell to any female wight.
You wavering crew, my curse to you I leave!
You had but one to give you any grace,
And you yourselves will Mariam's life bereave.   35
Your common-wealth doth innocency chase.
You creatures made to be the human curse,
You tigers, lionesses, hungry bears,
Tear massacring hyenas! Nay far worse,[1]
For they for prey do shed their feignèd tears.   40
But you will weep (you creatures cross[2] to good)
For your unquenchèd thirst of human blood.
You were the angels cast from heav'n for pride,
And still do keep your angels' outward show,
But none of you are inly beautified,   45
For still your heav'n-depriving pride doth grow.
Did not the sins of man require a scourge,
Your place on earth had been by this withstood,
But since a flood no more the world must purge,
You stayed in office[3] of a second flood.   50
You giddy creatures, sowers of debate,
You'll love today, and for no other cause,
But for you yesterday did deeply hate.
You are the wreck of order, breach of laws,
Your best are foolish, froward, wanton, vain;   55
Your worst adulterous, murderous, cunning, proud;
And Salome attends the latter train,
Or rather, she their leader is allowed.
I do the sottishness of men bewail,
That do with following you enhance your pride.   60
'Twere better that the human race should fail,

---

1   Hyenas produce tears whilst devouring their prey, which Constabarus initially uses
as an image of women's hypocrisy. But he then goes on to compound the accusation
by saying that women weep because their murderous appetites are never satisfied.

2   Hindrance.

3   To serve in place of.

Than be by such a mischief multiplied.
Cham's servile curse[1] to all your sex was given,
Because in Paradise you did offend.
Then do we not resist the will of Heaven,   65
When on your wills like servants we attend?
You are to nothing constant but to ill,
You are with nought but wickedness endued;
Your loves are set on nothing but your will,
And thus my censure I of you conclude: 70
You are the least of goods, the worst of evils,
Your best are worse than men, your worst than devils.
BABA'S 2 SON.   Come let us to our death. Are we not blessed?
Our death will freedom from these creatures give –
Those trouble-quiet sowers of unrest.   75
And this I vow: That had I leave to live,
I would for ever lead a single life,
And never venture on a devilish wife.   *(Exeunt)*

Scene vii

(Enter Herod and Salome)

HEROD.   Nay, she shall die.
SALOME.   Die quoth you?
HEROD.   That she shall!
But for the means, the means! Methinks 'tis hard
To find a means to murder her withal,
Therefore I am resolved she shall be spared.
SALOME.   Why, let her be beheaded.
HEROD.   That were well,   5
Think you that swords are miracles, like you?

---

1   This appears to be a conflation of more than one biblical curse, that of Eve, for
    her transgression in Eden, and also that of Ham, or Cham, who was cursed to
    servitude after bringing his brothers to observe their father Noah drunk and
    naked (Genesis 9:25, *Geneva*).

Her skin will ev'ry curtlax[1] edge refell,[2]
And then your enterprise you well may rue.
What if the fierce Arabian notice take,
Of this your wretched weaponless estate? 10
They answer, when we bid resistance make,
That Mariam's skin their fauchions did rebate.[3]
Beware of this, you make a goodly hand,
If you of weapons do deprive our land.
SALOME. Why drown her then.
HEROD.   Indeed a sweet device! 15
Why, would not every river turn her course
Rather than do her beauty prejudice,
And be reverted to the proper source?
So not a drop of water should be found
In all Judea's quondam[4] fertile ground. 20
SALOME. Then let the fire devour her.
HEROD.   'Twill not be.
Flame is from her derived into my heart.
Thou nursest flame, flame will not murder thee,
My fairest Mariam, fullest of desert.
SALOME. Then let her live for me.
HEROD.   Nay, she shall die. 25
But can you live without her?
SALOME.   Doubt you that?
HEROD. I'm sure I cannot. I beseech you try.
I have experience but I know not what.
SALOME. How should I try?
HEROD.   Why let my love be slain,
But if we cannot live without her sight 30
You'll find the means to make her breathe again,
Or else you will bereave my comfort quite.

---

1   Variant of curtle-ax, a form of cutlass.
2   Repel.
3   Blunt.
4   Previously.

SALOME. Oh aye, I warrant you. *(Exit)*
HEROD.   What, is she gone,
And gone to bid the world be overthrown?
What, is her heart's composure hardest stone?   35
To what a pass are cruel women grown?   *(Enter Salome)*
She is returned already. Have you done?
Is't possible you can command so soon
A creature's heart to quench the flaming sun,
Or from the sky to wipe away the moon?   40
SALOME. If Mariam be the sun and moon, it is,
For I already have commanded this.
HEROD. But have you seen her cheek?
SALOME.   A thousand times.
HEROD. But did you mark it too?
SALOME.   Aye, very well.
HEROD. What is't?
SALOME.   A crimson[1] bush[2] that ever limes[3]   45
The soul whose foresight doth not much excel.
HEROD. Send word she shall not die. Her cheek a bush!
Nay then I see indeed you marked it not.
SALOME. 'Tis very fair, but yet will never blush,
Though foul dishonours do her forehead blot.   50
HEROD. Then let her die, 'tis very true indeed,
And for this fault alone shall Mariam bleed.
SALOME. What fault my lord?
HEROD.   What fault is't? You that ask?
If you be ignorant I know of none.
To call her back from death shall be your task.   55
I'm glad that she for innocent is known.
For on the brow of Mariam hangs a fleece,[4]

---

1   The colour of Mariam's complexion, possibly with the implication that it is rouged.
2   The commercial symbol of the vintner. A bush was hung over the doorways of the vintner's premises to advertise the sale of wine. From this developed the phrase "to hang out bushes," which referred to women making themselves attractive or available.
3   A reference to catching with birdlime. This sticky substance was put on trees and bushes to catch birds.
4   Hair, with a probable reference to the Golden Fleece of Colchis.

Whose slenderest twine is strong enough to bind
The hearts of kings. The pride and shame of Greece,
Troy-flaming Helen's,[1] not so fairly shined. 60

SALOME. 'Tis true indeed, she lays them out for nets,
To catch the hearts that do not shun a bait.
'Tis time to speak, for Herod sure forgets
That Mariam's very tresses hide deceit.

HEROD. Oh do they so? Nay, then you do but well! 65
In sooth I thought it had been hair.
Nets call you them? Lord, how they do excel!
I never saw a net that showed so fair.
But have you heard her speak?

SALOME. You know I have.

HEROD. And were you not amazed?

SALOME. No, not a whit. 70

HEROD. Then 'twas not her you heard. Her life I'll save,
For Mariam hath a world-amazing wit.

SALOME. She speaks a beauteous language, but within
Her heart is false as powder[2] and her tongue
Doth but allure the auditors to sin, 75
And is the instrument to do you wrong.

HEROD. It may be so. Nay, 'tis so! She's unchaste!
Her mouth will ope to ev'ry stranger's ear.
Then let the executioner make haste,
Lest she enchant him, if her words he hear. 80
Let him be deaf, lest she do him surprise,
That shall to free her spirit be assigned.
Yet what boots deafness if he have his eyes?
Her murderer must be both deaf and blind,
For if he see, he needs must see the stars 85

---

1   A reference to Helen's effect on Troy – that it was eventually burnt down as a
     result of her seduction by Paris. Perhaps also, there is an implicit reference to the
     lines in *Dr. Faustus*, "Was this the face that launched a thousand ships / And
     burnt the topless towers of Ilium?" (xii.81-82)
2   Possibly a reference to cosmetics, meaning her heart is as false as a painted face.

That shine on either side of Mariam's face,
Whose sweet aspect will terminate the wars;
Wherewith he should a soul so precious chase?
Her eyes can speak, and in their speaking move.
Oft did my heart with reverence receive   90
The world's mandates. Pretty tales of love
They utter, which can human bondage weave.
But shall I let this heaven's model die,
Which for a small self-portraiture she drew?
Her eyes like stars, her forehead like the sky,   95
She is like heaven, and must be heavenly true.
SALOME. Your thoughts do rave with doting on the Queen.
Her eyes are ebon[1]-hewed, and you'll confess
A sable[2] star hath been but seldom seen.
Then speak of reason more, of Mariam less.   100
HEROD. Yourself are held a goodly creature here,
Yet so unlike my Mariam in your shape,
That when to her you have approachèd near,
Myself hath often ta'en you for an ape;
And yet you prate[3] of beauty! Go your ways,   105
You are to her a sunburnt blackamoor!
Your paintings[4] cannot equal Mariam's praise:
Her nature is so rich, you are so poor.
Let her be stayed from death, for if she die,
We do we know not what to stop her breath.   110
A world cannot another Mariam buy.
Why stay you ling'ring? Countermand her death.
SALOME. Then you'll no more remember what hath passed.
Sohemus' love and hers shall be forgot.
'Tis well in truth, that fault may be her last,   115
And she may mend, though yet she loves you not.

---

1   Ebony.
2   Heraldic term for black.
3   Chatter.
4   Cosmetic enhancements.

HEROD. Oh God, 'tis true! Sohemus! Earth and heav'n,
Why did you both conspire to make me cursed
In coz'ning me with shows, and proofs unev'n?
She showed the best, and yet did prove the worst.   120
Her show was such, as had our singing king,[1]
The holy David, Mariam's beauty seen,
The Hittite had then felt no deadly sting,
Nor Bethsabe had never been a queen.[2]
Or had his son, the wisest man of men,[3]   125
Whose fond delight did most consist in change,[4]
Beheld her face, he had been stayed again;
No creature having her, can wish to range.
Had Asuerus seen my Mariam's brow,
The humble Jew,[5] she might have walked alone.   130
Her beauteous virtue should have stayed below,
Whiles Mariam mounted to the Persian throne.
But what avails it all? For in the weight
She is deceitful, light as vanity!
Oh she was made for nothing but a bait   135
To train some hapless man to misery.
I am the hapless man that have been trained
To endless bondage. I will see her yet!
Methinks I should discern her if she feigned.
Can human eyes be dazed by woman's wit?   140
Once more these eyes of mine with hers shall meet
Before the headsman do her life bereave.
Shall I forever part from thee, my sweet,
Without the taking of my latest leave?

---

1 David, author of the Psalms.
2 King David committed adultery with Bethsabe, the wife of Uriah the Hittite.
   She became pregnant as a result. David arranged to put Uriah in the forefront of
   the battle at the seige of Rabbath, in the hope that he would be killed. When this
   plan proved successful, David married Bethsabe (2 Samuel 11, *Geneva*).
3 Solomon.
4 Solomon "had seven hundreth wives that were princesses and three hundreth
   concubines" (1 Kings 11:3, *Geneva*).
5 Esther, the eponymous heroine of the Old Testament book of Esther. She became
   the second wife of King Asuerus, or Artaxerxes, who chose her for her great beauty.

SALOME. You had as good resolve to save her now!   145
  I'll stay her death, 'tis well determinèd.
  For sure she never more will break her vow,
  Sohemus and Josephus are both dead.
HEROD. She shall not live, nor will I see her face.
  A long healed wound, a second time doth bleed!   150
  With Joseph I remember her disgrace,
  A shameful end ensues a shameful deed.
  Oh that I had not called to mind anew
  The discontent of Mariam's wavering heart.
  'Twas you! You foul mouthed Ate,[1] none but you   155
  That did the thought hereof to me impart.
  Hence from my sight, my black tormentor hence!
  For hadst thou not made Herod unsecure
  I had not doubted Mariam's innocence,
  But still had held her in my heart for pure.   160
SALOME. I'll leave you to your passion. 'Tis no time
  To purge me now, though of a guiltless crime.   *(Exit)*
HEROD. Destruction take thee! Thou hast made my heart
  As heavy as revenge. I am so dull,
  Methinks I am not sensible of smart,   165
  Though hideous horrors at my bosom pull.
  My head weighs downwards, therefore will I go
  To try if I can sleep away my woe.   *(Exit)*

Scene viii

(Enter Mariam)

MARIAM. Am I the Mariam that presumed so much,
  And deemed my face must needs preserve my breath?
  Aye, I it was that thought my beauty such,
  As it alone could countermand my death.

---

1   Daughter of Zeus and goddess of evil.

Now death will teach me: he can pale as well   5
A cheek of roses, as a cheek less bright,
And dim an eye whose shine doth most excel,
As soon as one that casts a meaner light.
Had not myself against myself conspired,
No plot, no adversary from without,   10
Could Herod's love from Mariam have retired,
Or from his heart have thrust my semblance out.
The wanton Queen that never loved for love,
False Cleopatra, wholly set on gain,
With all her sleights did prove,[1] yet vainly prove,   15
For her the love of Herod to obtain.
Yet her allurements, all her courtly guile,
Her smiles, her favours, and her smooth deceit,
Could not my face from Herod's mind exile,
But were with him of less than little weight.   20
That face and person that in Asia late
For beauty's goddess, Paphos' Queen,[2] was ta'en,
That face that did captive great Julius' fate,
That very face that was Antonius' bane,
That face that to be Egypt's pride was born,   25
That face that all the world esteemed so rare,
Did Herod hate, despise, neglect, and scorn,
When with the same he Mariam's did compare.[3]
This made that I improvidently[4] wrought,
And on the wager even my life did pawn,   30
Because I thought, and yet but truly thought,
That Herod's love could not from me be drawn.
But now, though out of time, I plainly see
It could be drawn, though never drawn[5] from me.
Had I but with humility been graced,   35

---

1   Try.
2   Venus. According to legend, she was born out of the sea off the shores of Paphos.
3   Cleopatra's attempted seduction of Herod is detailed by Josephus (*Ant.*, 389).
4   Imprudently, unwisely.
5   In the first instance, "taken away," in the second, "manipulated."

As well as fair I might have proved me wise,
But I did think because I knew me chaste,
One virtue for a woman might suffice.
That mind for glory of our sex might stand,
Wherein humility and chastity   40
Do march with equal paces hand in hand.[1]
But if one single seen, who setteth by?
And I had singly one, but 'tis my joy,
That I was ever innocent, though sour,
And therefore can they but my life destroy;   45
My soul is free from adversary's power.

(Enter Doris, unseen by Mariam)

You princes great in power and high in birth,
Be great and high, I envy not your hap.
Your birth must be from dust, your power on earth,
In heav'n shall Mariam sit in Sara's[2] lap.   50
DORIS. In heav'n! Your beauty cannot bring you thither.
Your soul is black and spotted, full of sin.
You in adult'ry lived nine years together,
And heav'n will never let adult'ry in.
MARIAM. What art thou that dost poor Mariam pursue?   55
Some spirit sent to drive me to despair?
Who sees for truth that Mariam is untrue?
If fair she be, she is as chaste as fair.
DORIS. I am that Doris that was once beloved,
Beloved by Herod, Herod's lawful wife.   60
'Twas you that Doris from his side removed,
And robbed from me the glory of my life.

---

1 Lines 39-42 refer to the fact that women are expected to exhibit humility as well
as chastity. Mariam is saying that the woman whose mind comprises chastity and
humility would be considered "the glory of our sex," whereas no one would be
particularly impressed by a woman like Mariam, who exhibits only one of the
two virtues.

2 Wife of Abraham and "mother" of the Jewish race (Genesis 12:10-14, *Geneva*).
Sara's lap may be taken as a female equivalent of Abraham's bosom, denoting
heaven or the after-life.

MARIAM. Was that adult'ry? Did not Moses say
    That he that being matched did deadly hate,
    Might by permission put his wife away   65
    And take a more beloved to be his mate?
DORIS. What did he hate me for? For simple truth?
    For bringing beauteous babes for love to him?
    For riches, noble birth, or tender youth,
    Or for no stain did Doris' honour dim?   70
    Oh tell me Mariam, tell me if you know,
    Which fault of these made Herod Doris' foe.
    These thrice three years have I with hands held up,
    And bowèd knees fast nailèd to the ground,
    Besought for thee the dregs of that same cup,   75
    That cup of wrath[1] that is for sinners found,
    And now thou art to drink it! Doris' curse
    Upon thyself did all this while attend,
    But now it shall pursue thy children worse.
MARIAM. Oh Doris, now to thee my knees I bend,   80
    That heart that never bowed, to thee doth bow.
    Curse not mine infants, let it thee suffice,
    That Heav'n doth punishment to me allow.
    Thy curse is cause that guiltless Mariam dies.
DORIS. Had I ten thousand tongues, and ev'ry tongue   85
    Inflamed with poison's power and steeped in gall,
    My curses would not answer for my wrong,
    Though I in cursing thee employed them all.
    Hear thou that didst mount Gerarim[2] command
    To be a place whereon with cause to curse,   90
    Stretch thy revenging arm, thrust forth thy hand,

---

1   See Jeremiah 25:9-38, *Geneva*.
2   Possibly Mount Gerizim, over which Moses was given command by God: "When
    the Lord thy God therefore hathe broght thee into the land, whether thou goest to
    possesse it then thou shalt put the blesing upon Mount Gerizim and the curse
    upon Mount Ebal" (Deuteronomy 11:29, *Geneva*). Cerasano and Wynne-Davies
    (194) point out that Gerazim (their spelling), according to Samaritan tradition, was
    the mountain upon which Abraham was instructed to sacrifice Isaac. As the focus
    of Doris' curse is Mariam's offspring, the reference would appear to be appropriate.

And plague the mother much, the children worse.
Throw flaming fire upon the baseborn heads
That were begotten in unlawful beds.
But let them live till they have sense to know   95
What 'tis to be in miserable state;
Then be their nearest friends their overthrow,
Attended be they by suspicious hate.
And Mariam, I do hope this boy of mine
Shall one day come to be the death of thine.   *(Exit)* 100
MARIAM.   Oh, Heaven forbid! I hope the world shall see
This curse of thine shall be returned on thee!
Now earth farewell, though I be yet but young,
Yet I, methinks, have known thee too, too long.   *(Exit)*

CHORUS.

The fairest action of our human life,
Is scorning to revenge an injury;
For who forgives without a further strife,
His adversary's heart to him doth tie.
    And 'tis a firmer conquest truly said,   5
    To win the heart, than overthrow the head.

If we a worthy enemy do find,
To yield to worth, it must be nobly done;
But if of baser metal be his mind,
In base revenge there is no honour won.   10
    Who would a worthy courage overthrow,
    And who would wrestle with a worthless foe?

We say our hearts are great and cannot yield,
Because they cannot yield it proves them poor;
Great hearts are tasked beyond their power but seld.[1]   15
The weakest lions will the loudest roar.

---

1   Seldom.

Truth's school for certain doth this same allow,
High heartedness doth sometimes teach to bow.

A noble heart doth teach a virtuous scorn,
To scorn to owe a duty over-long,   20
To scorn to be for benefits forborn,
To scorn to lie, to scorn to do a wrong,
 To scorn to bear an injury in mind,
 To scorn a free-born heart slave-like to bind.

But if for wrongs we needs revenge must have,   25
Then be our vengeance of the noblest kind.
Do we his body from our fury save,
And let our hate prevail against his mind?
 What can 'gainst him a greater vengeance be,
 Than make his foe more worthy far than he?   30

Had Mariam scorned to leave a due unpaid,
She would to Herod then have paid her love,
And not have been by sullen passion swayed.
To fix her thoughts all injury above
 Is virtuous pride. Had Mariam thus been proud, 35
 Long famous life to her had been allowed.

ACT V

Scene i

(Enter Nuntio)

NUNTIO. When, sweetest friend, did I so far offend
    Your heavenly self, that you my fault to quit
    Have made me now relator of her end,
    The end of beauty, chastity and wit?
    Was none so hapless in the fatal place   5
    But I, most wretched, for the Queen to choose?
    'Tis certain I have some ill boding face
    That made me culled to tell this luckless news.
    And yet no news to Herod. Were it new
    To him, unhappy 'thad not been at all.   10
    Yet do I long to come within his view,
    That he may know his wife did guiltless fall.
    And here he comes. Your Mariam greets you well.

(Enter Herod)

HEROD. What, lives my Mariam? Joy, exceeding joy!
    She shall not die.
NUNTIO. Heav'n doth your will repel.   15
HEROD. Oh do not with thy words my life destroy!
    I prithee tell no dying-tale. Thine eye
    Without thy tongue doth tell but too, too much.
    Yet let thy tongue's addition make me die,
    Death welcome comes to him whose grief is such.   20
NUNTIO. I went amongst the curious gazing troop,
    To see the last of her that was the best,
    To see if death had heart to make her stoop,
    To see the sun admiring Phoenix'[1] nest.
    When there I came, upon the way I saw   25

---

1   A mythical bird, perpetually re-born from the ashes of its own funeral pyre,
   which was ignited when the sun stopped its course in the heavens to admire the
   Phoenix's beauty.

The stately Mariam not debased by fear;
Her look did seem to keep the world in awe,
Yet mildly did her face this fortune bear.
HEROD. Thou dost usurp my right! My tongue was framed
To be the instrument of Mariam's praise.   30
Yet speak. She cannot be too often famed;
All tongues suffice not her sweet name to raise.
NUNTIO. But as she came she Alexandra met,
Who did her death (sweet Queen) no whit bewail,
But as if nature she did quite forget,   35
She did upon her daughter loudly rail.
HEROD. Why stopped you not her mouth? Where had she words
To darken that, that Heaven made so bright?
Our sacred tongue[1] no epithet affords,
To call her other than the world's delight.   40
NUNTIO. She told her that her death was too, too good,
And that already she had lived too long;
She said she shamed to have a part in blood
Of her that did the princely Herod wrong.
HEROD. Base pick-thank[2] devil! Shame? 'Twas all her glory,   45
That she to noble Mariam was the mother!
But never shall it live in any story
Her name, except to infamy, I'll smother.
What answer did her princely daughter make?
NUNTIO. She made no answer, but she looked the while,   50
As if thereof she scarce did notice take,
Yet smiled a dutiful, though scornful, smile.
HEROD. Sweet creature, I that look to mind do call;
Full oft hath Herod been amazed withal.
Go on.
NUNTIO. She came unmoved with pleasant grace,   55
As if to triumph her arrival were,
In stately habit, and with cheerful face,
Yet ev'ry eye was moist, but Mariam's there.

---

1   Herod may be referring to his own tongue or to the sacred language of Hebrew.
2   One who curries favour.

When justly opposite to me she came,
She picked me out from all the crew.   60
She beckoned to me, called me by my name,
For she my name, my birth, and fortune knew.
HEROD.   What, did she name thee? Happy, happy man!
Wilt thou not ever love that name the better?
But what sweet tune did this fair dying swan[1]   65
Afford thine ear? Tell all, omit no letter.
NUNTIO.   Tell thou my lord, said she –
HEROD.   Me, meant she me?
Is't true? The more my shame, I was her lord,
Were I not made her lord, I still should be,
But now her name must be by me adored.   70
Oh say, what said she more? Each word she said
Shall be the food whereon my heart is fed.
NUNTIO.   Tell thou my lord thou sawst me lose my breath.
HEROD.   Oh that I could that sentence now control!
NUNTIO.   If guiltily eternal be my death.   75
HEROD.   I hold her chaste ev'n in my inmost soul!
NUNTIO.   By three days hence, if wishes could revive,
I know himself would make me oft alive.
HEROD.   Three days? Three hours, three minutes, not so much:
A minute in a thousand parts divided!   80
My penitency for her death is such,
As in the first I wished she had not died.
But forward in thy tale.
NUNTIO.   Why on she went,
And after she some silent prayer had said,
She died as if to die she were content,   85
And thus to heav'n her heav'nly soul is fled.
HEROD.   But art thou sure there doth no life remain?
Is't possible my Mariam should be dead?
Is there no trick to make her breathe again?
NUNTIO.   Her body is divided from her head.   90

---

1   Swans were reputed to sing before they died.

HEROD. Why yet methinks there might be found, by art,
    Strange ways of cure. 'Tis sure rare things are done
    By an inventive head, and willing heart.
NUNTIO. Let not, my lord, your fancies idly run.
    It is as possible it should be seen   95
    That we should make the holy Abraham live,
    Though he entombed two thousand years had been,
    As breath again to slaughtered Mariam give.
    But now for more assaults prepare your ears.
HEROD. There cannot be a further cause of moan;   100
    This accident shall shelter me from fears.
    What can I fear? Already Mariam's gone.
    Yet tell ev'n what you will.
NUNTIO.   As I came by
    From Mariam's death, I saw, upon a tree,
    A man that to his neck a cord did tie,   105
    Which cord he had designed his end to be.
    When me he once discerned, he downwards bowed,
    And thus with fearful voice he cried aloud,
    "Go tell the King he trusted ere he tried,[1]
    I am the cause that Mariam causeless died!"   110
HEROD. Damnation take him, for it was the slave
    That said she meant with poison's deadly force
    To end my life, that she the crown might have,
    Which tale did Mariam from herself divorce.
    Oh pardon me thou pure unspotted ghost!   115
    My punishment must needs sufficient be,
    In missing that content I valued most,
    Which was thy admirable face to see.
    I had but one inestimable jewel,
    Yet one I had, no monarch had the like,   120
    And therefore may I curse myself as cruel,
    'Twas broken by a blow myself did strike.

---

1   Herod trusted the words of others before trying to find out the truth. Cf. Chorus
    II, stanza 1.

I gazed thereon and never thought me blessed,
But when on it my dazzled eye might rest.
A precious mirror made by wondrous art,   125
I prized it ten times dearer than my crown,
And laid it up fast folded in my heart,
Yet I in sudden choler cast it down
And pashed[1] it all to pieces. 'Twas no foe
That robbed me of it, no Arabian host,[2]   130
Nor no Armenian guide[3] hath used me so,
But Herod's wretched self hath Herod crossed
She was my graceful moi'ty,[4] me accursed,
To slay my better half and save my worst.
But sure she is not dead? You did but jest,   135
To put me in perplexity a while.
'Twere well indeed if I could so be 'dressed,
I see she is alive, methinks you smile.

NUNTIO.   If sainted Abel[5] yet deceasèd be,
'Tis certain Mariam is as dead as he.   140

HEROD.   Why then go call her to me, bid her now
Put on fair habit, stately ornament,
And let no frown o'ershade her smoothest brow,
In her doth Herod place his whole content.

NUNTIO.   She'll come in stately weeds to please your sense,   145
If now she come attired in robe of heaven.
Remember you yourself did send her hence,
And now to you she can no more be given.

HEROD.   She's dead! Hell take her murderers! She was fair.
Oh what a hand she had, it was so white,   150
It did the whiteness of the snow impair.
I never more shall see so sweet a sight.

---

1   Smashed.
2   Arabian army. The play contains other references to the strained relations between
    Arabia and Palestine. Cf. II.iv and I.vii.
3   Perhaps a reference to the duplicity of Armenia Minor which remained sympathatic
    to the Parthians, whilst professing allegiance to Rome.
4   Contraction of moiety, a portion or share.
5   The second son of Adam, murdered by his brother, Cain.

NUNTIO. 'Tis true, her hand was rare.

HEROD.   Her hand? Her hands!
    She had not singly one of beauty rare,
    But such a pair as here where Herod stands,   155
    He dares the world to make to both compare.
    Accursèd Salome! Hadst thou been still,
    My Mariam had been breathing by my side.
    Oh never had I, had I had my will,
    Sent forth command that Mariam should have died.   160
    But Salome thou didst with envy vex,
    To see thyself out-matchèd in thy sex.
    Upon your sex's forehead Mariam sat,
    To grace you all like an imperial crown,
    But you, fond fool, have rudely pushed thereat,   165
    And proudly pulled your proper glory down.
    One smile of hers – nay not so much – a look
    Was worth a hundred thousand such as you.
    Judea how canst thou the wretches brook,
    That robbed from thee the fairest of the crew?   170
    You dwellers in the now deprivèd land,
    Wherein the matchless Mariam was bred,
    Why grasp not each of you a sword in hand,
    To aim at me, your cruel sovereign's head?
    Oh when you think of Herod as your King,   175
    And owner of the pride of Palestine,
    This act to your remembrance likewise bring,
    'Tis I have overthrown your royal line.
    Within her purer veins the blood did run,
    That from her grandam¹ Sara she derived,   180
    Whose beldam age the love of kings hath won.
    Oh that her issue had as long been lived!
    But can her eye be made by death obscure?
    I cannot think but it must sparkle still,
    Foul sacrilege to rob those lights so pure,   185

---

1   Female ancestor.

From out a temple made by heav'nly skill.
I am the villain that have done the deed,
The cruel deed, though by another's hand;
My word though not my sword made Mariam bleed.
Hircanus' grandchild died at my command;   190
That Mariam that I once did love so dear,
The partner of my now detested bed.
Why shine you sun with an aspect so clear?
I tell you once again my Mariam's dead.
You could but shine, if some Egyptian blowse,[1]   195
Or Ethiopian dowdy[2] lose her life.
This was (then wherefore bend you not your brows?)
The King of Jewry's fair and spotless wife.
Deny thy beams, and moon refuse thy light,
Let all the stars be dark, let Jewry's eye   200
No more distinguish which is day and night,
Since her best birth did in her bosom die.
Those fond idolaters, the men of Greece,
Maintain these orbs are safely governèd,
That each within themselves have gods apiece   205
By whom their steadfast course is justly led.[3]
But were it so, as so it cannot be,
They all would put their mourning garments on.
Not one of them would yield a light to me,
To me that is the cause that Mariam's gone.   210
For though they fame their Saturn[4] melancholy,
Of sour behaviours, and of angry mood,
They fame him likewise to be just and holy,
And justice needs must seek revenge for blood.

---

1 A red-faced woman.
2 A shabby, slatternly woman.
3 Each planet is controlled by a single deity. In the ensuing passage, Herod randomly
   calls the gods by their Greek and/or Roman names.
4 Roman name for Cronos, ruler of the gods until usurped by his son Zeus. The
   planet was associated with wisdom and melancholy.

Their Jove,[1] if Jove he were, would sure desire   215
To punish him that slew so fair a lass,
For Leda's[2] beauty set his heart on fire,
Yet she not half so fair as Mariam was.
And Mars[3] would deem his Venus[4] had been slain,
Sol[5] to recover her would never stick,   220
For if he want the power her life to gain,
Then physic's god[6] is but an empiric.[7]
The Queen of love[8] would storm for beauty's sake,
And Hermes[9] too, since he bestowed her wit,
The night's pale light[10] for angry grief would shake,   225
To see chaste Mariam die in age unfit.
But oh, I am deceived, she passed them all
In every gift, in every property;
Her excellencies wrought her timeless fall,
And they rejoiced, not grieved, to see her die.   230
The Paphian goddess[11] did repent her waste,
When she to one such beauty did allow;
Mercurius thought her wit his wit surpassed,
And Cynthia[12] envied Mariam's brighter brow.
But these are fictions, they are void of sense,   235
The Greeks but dream, and dreaming, falsehoods tell;
They neither can offend nor give defence,
And not by them it was my Mariam fell.

---

1   Ruler of the gods, alternatively known as Zeus in Greek mythology, or Jupiter in
    Roman mythology.
2   Wife of King Tyndareus of Sparta. She was seduced by Jove in the shape of a
    swan, and bore him two sons, Castor and Pollux.
3   Roman god of war, called Ares in Greek mythology.
4   Roman goddess of love, called Aphrodite in Greek mythology.
5   The sun.
6   Apollo, who was the god of medicine as well as the god of the sun.
7   An untrained practitioner or quack.
8   Venus.
9   Messenger of the gods and famed for his wit, called Mercury in Roman mythology.
10 The moon.
11 Venus.
12 Goddess of the moon, alternatively known as Artemis in Greek mythology and
    Diana in Roman mythology.

If she had been like an Egyptian black,
And not so fair, she had been longer lived. 240
Her overflow of beauty turnèd back,
And drowned the spring from whence it was derived.
Her heav'nly beauty 'twas that made me think
That it with chastity could never dwell,
But now I see that Heav'n in her did link 245
A spirit and a person to excel.
I'll muffle up myself in endless night,
And never let mine eyes behold the light.
Retire thyself, vile monster, worse than he
That stained the virgin earth with brother's blood,[1] 250
Still in some vault or den enclosèd be,
Where with thy tears thou may'st beget a flood,
Which flood in time may drown thee. Happy day,
When thou at once shalt die and find a grave.
A stone upon the vault, someone shall lay, 255
Which monument shall an inscription have,
And these shall be the words it shall contain:
"Here Herod lies, that hath his Mariam slain."

CHORUS.

Who ever hath beheld with steadfast eye,
The strange events of this one only day?
How many were deceived, how many die,
That once today did grounds of safety lay?
It will from them all certainty bereave, 5
Since twice six hours so many can deceive.

This morning Herod held for surely dead,
And all the Jews on Mariam did attend,
And Constabarus rise from Salom's bed,
And neither dreamed of a divorce or end. 10

---

1   Cain, who slew his brother Abel (Genesis 4:8-16, *Geneva*).

Pheroras joyed that he might have his wife,
And Baba's sons for safety of their life.

Tonight our Herod doth alive remain, A
The guiltless Mariam is deprived of breath, B
Stout Constabarus both divorced and slain, A 15
The valiant sons of Baba have their death. B
    Pheroras sure his love to be bereft, C
    If Salome her suit unmade had left, C

Herod this morning did expect with joy,
To see his Mariam's much belovèd face 20
And yet ere night he did her life destroy,
And surely thought she did her name disgrace.
    Yet now again so short do humours[1] last,
    He both repents her death and knows her chaste.

Had he with wisdom now her death delayed, 25
He at his pleasure might command her death,
But now he hath his power so much betrayed,
As all his woes cannot restore her breath,
    Now doth he strangely lunaticly rave
    Because his Mariam's life he cannot save. 30

This day's events were certainly ordained,
To be the warning to posterity,
So many changes are therein contained,
So admirably strange variety.
    This day alone, our sagest Hebrews shall 35
    In after times the school of wisdom call.

FINIS

---

1   Moods.

Emendations and Variant Readings

This list serves to indicate the major emendations I have made to the original 1613 text, and also to compare alternative emendations by other editors. Where only the original 1613 text is listed, the other editions retain this or use the same emendation.

The following abbreviations apply:

sp.n. (speaker's name)
s.d. (stage direction)
MS (manuscript emendation)

The Names of the Speakers

5   his son by Doris] 1613, his sonne by Salome.

11   Baba's] 1613, Babus.

16   Butler] 1613, Bu. This expansion is suggested by Lodge's translation of Josephus, in which the treacherous servant is referred to as a butler (*Ant.*, 398).

18   Silleus' man] 1613, not listed.

19   Soldiers] 1613, not listed.

20   Attendants] 1613, not listed.

The Argument

3   daughter] 1613, daughrer; Purkiss 1994, grandaughter.

5   repudiated] 1613, reputiated.

22   bore] 1613, bare.

23   exceeding hardly] Purkiss 1994, Cerasano and Wynne-Davies, exceedingly hard.

36   this] Bod.M MS, the.

I.i.1-4 There are a variety of ways in which this opening quatrain may be punctuated. 1613 and Purkiss 1994 have a question mark at the end of the first line, but the syntax indicates that the sentence is longer. Cerasano and Wynne-Davies put the question mark at the end of the third line; Weller and Ferguson and Gutierrez do not employ a question mark at all, although there is clearly the need for one at some point.

I.i.10 Line is two syllables short] Huntington MS, One object onely yeelds; Dyce MS, yeelds to me both.

I.i.32 bore] 1613, bare.

I.i.35 loveliest] 1613, lowlyest Dunstan, Dyce MS and Weller and Ferguson, loveliest; Cerasano and Wynne-Davies and Gutierrez, lowliest.

I.i.39 Why joy I not the tongue no more shall speak] Cerasano and Wynne-Davies, Why joy I not? The tongue no more shall speak.

I.i.44 ascent] 1613, assent.

I.i.45 he murdered thee] Purkiss 1994, he murdered he.

I.i.47 mind] 1613, maide. A misprint for mind which makes the rhyme with find. No maid appears in the play or in the source, both of which state that Sohemus told Mariam himself (IV. iii; *Ant.*, 397).

I.i.67 Aye] 1613, I.

I.i.68 your admirer and my lord.] 1613, your admirer. And my Lord.

I.i.71 bore] 1613, bare.

I.ii.3 murd'rer's] 1613, murther's; Dunstan, Cerasano and Wynne-Davies, murthrer's.

I.ii.12 famed] 1613, fain'd.

I.ii.44 Herod] 1613, Mariam. Probably a printer's error. The substitution of sp.n. Nun: for sp.n. Mar: later in this scene and the omission of sp.n. Mar: in III. iii showns that errors of this nature were not uncommon. According to Weller and Ferguson (155): "It is, however, possible to understand 'Mariam' as an indirect object ('Was it love that gave a death sentence to Mariam?'), rather than as a subject of 'gave commandment'." PM MS, "Mariam" underlined, "Herod?" in the margin.

I.ii.53 sp.n. Mariam] 1613, sp.n. Nun: No Nuntio is listed at the beginning of the scene or makes an entrance up to this point.

I.ii.55 If] Dunstan, Weller and Ferguson and Gutierrez, Of. Weller and Ferguson's emendation gives the sense that the coals of Doris' love were raked up in the embers of Mariam's. With "If" retained, the sense is slightly more obscure, but reads "If Herod were to reject Mariam, he would not return to Doris, as his love for her died out long ago."

I.ii.93 sleight] 1613, slight. The context obviously refers to cunning rather than insult which is the usual meaning of "slight." The 1613 text has no consistent spelling, giving "slite" at later points in the text, for both meanings. In this edition, spelling has been standardized the to "sleight" or "slight" depending on the context.

I.ii.104 seek] 1613, leeke Dyce MS, Weller and Ferguson and Cerasano and Wynne-Davies, like. Weller and Ferguson suggest (156), that the spelling "may merely reflect contemporary pronunciation of like." However, it is also possible that the printer mistook Cary's long "s" for an "l."

I.ii.107 bar] 1613, bare Cerasano and Wynne-Davies bear. My emendation has been made to give the sense of prevent or exclude, although the meanings of "to strip" or "to carry away" could also apply here.

I.ii.120 And part] Dyce MS, And past; Dunstan Apart.

I.iii.11 discontent] Dunstan, Cerasano and Wynne-Davies discontents. Cerasano and Wynne-Davies emend to retain the rhyme scheme.

I.iii.13 rein] 1613, raine.

I.iii.22 choler] 1613, collor.

I.iii.47 suspicion's] 1613, suspitious; Dunstan suspition's.

I.iii.50 Joseph's] 1613, Josephus. The extra syllable has been removed for the sake of the meter.

I.iv.16 all eyes] 1613, allyes.

I.iv.20 Arabian's bride] 1613, Arabian Bride.

I.iv.38 from] 1613, for. This was possibly meant to be printed as fro, the form used in 1613, II. ii.

I.iv.39 principles] Purkiss 1994, principle.

I.iv.45 men] 1613, man. "Men" agrees with the other references, which are in the plural form, and also reinforces the gender specificity of the term.

I.v.4 O more] 1613, a more.

I.v.15 do's] 1613, do'es; Gutierrez do is. The meaning is evidently "do is," but the words must be elided into one syllable in order to retain the meter.

I.v.30 not aught] 1613, not ought; Dunstan on ought. Dunstan's emendation implies that Silleus lacked, rather than possessed, influence over Obodas.

I.v.37 whom] 1613, home; Purkiss 1998, whome.

I.vi.25 forfeited to haples] 1613, forfeited haples; Cerasano and Wynne-Davies forfeited? Hapless fate; Bod.M forfeited? Oh hapless fate; Purkiss 1994, forfeited? – hapless fate.

I.vi.32 Use makes] 1613, Use make; Purkiss 1994, Use made.

I.vi.51 beasts swim] 1613, beasts, swine.

I.vi.56 water-bearing] 1613, waters-bearing.

I.vi.79 precedent] 1613, president.

I.vi.90 vow] 1613, vowd.

I.vi.96 s.d. Exit] 1613, no s.d.

I.vi.118 s.d. Exit] 1613, no s.d.

Ch.I.8 leap] 1613, lep.

Ch.I.9 If] 1613, Of.

II.i.12 monarchal] 1613, monachall.

II.i.24 teach us blood] 1613, teach blood; Dyce MS, teach both blood. Bod.M displays a caret between "blood" and "kindreds" indicating an omission.

II.i.41 speakst] 1613, speaks; Cerasano and Wynne-Davies, speak.

II.i.63 best] Dunstan, lest. The tone of the scene is one which rejects social status in favour of love. It would be out of context for Graphina to prize Pheroras' love the most because he rejected a princess for her. Rather, Graphina's words mean that she is not saving the best till last, which is the meaning resulting from Dunstan's emendation.

II.i.73 needs not. Let Graphina] 1613, needs not let Graphina. I concur with Cerasano and Wynne-Davies's emendation. All other editors retain the 1613 punctuation.

II.i.80 holds the glory] Bod.M MS and Dyce MS, holds thee, glory.

II.ii.20 others, right] 1613, others right; Purkiss 1994, other's right.

II.ii.34 quick buried. You had] 1613, quick buried, you had; Weller and Ferguson quick buried; you had.

II.ii.39 overpassed] 1613, operpast. Probably a printer's error. The *OED* does not list "operpast." However, it does list the word "opertaneous," now obsolete, from the Latin "opert-us" (covered) and "ane-us" (belonging to the class of), meaning secret, hidden or covert nature. It is possible that "operpast" is in some way related to this word and means "spent in hiding," as the context would suggest.

II.ii.48 safety] 1613, safely. Dunstan suggests "saftey," which I have followed because Baba's 2 son's particular concern for Constabarus is in keeping with his use of the cuckoo metaphor.

II.ii.66 fear] 1613, leare; Purkiss 1994, leer.

II.ii.87 Constabarus] 1613, Constab: A typographical abbreviation, occurring several times in the text. The metre demands that the full name be spoken.

II.ii.93 live] Dunstan, Weller and Ferguson, Purkiss 1994, Cerasano and Wynne-Davies and Purkis 1998, lie. This emendation would make the rhyme, although it is not necessary for the sense.

II.ii.98 Julius'] 1613, Julions; Cerasano and Wynne-Davies Julian's.

II.ii.102 phys'nomy] 1613, Phismony; Purkiss 1994 and Gutierrez, phisnomy; Cerasano and Wynne-Davies, physiognomy.

II.ii.114 to set] Cerasano and Wynne-Davies, so let; Gutierrez, to let.

II.iii.1 You . . . sides] 1613, Your . . . side; Weller and Ferguson, Purkiss 1994, Cerasano and Wynne-Davies and Gutierrez, You . . . side.

II.iii.11 stoop] 1613, scope. Cerasano and Wynne-Davies (194) gloss "scope" as "give room to her."

II.iii.23 lake] Weller and Ferguson and Gutierrez, lack.

II.iii.25 oaths] 1613, oath.

II.iv.9 exception] 1613, expectation.

II.iv.11 wielded] 1613, welded.

II.iv.51 wilt not] Cerasano and Wynne-Davies, will not.

II.iv.66 s.d. They fight] 1613, no s.d. All editors except Dunstan and Gutierrez agree that the fight begins here.

II.iv.92 s.d. They fight] 1613, I, I, they fight; Weller and Ferguson Ay, ay, They fight. The stage direction does not form part of the spoken text. Of the extant 1613 texts, E, PM, EC, Ho and Bod.M have MS markings which separate it from the spoken text. Weller and Ferguson suggest that "I, I" might represent the cries of the combatants, or may be the printer's corruption of parentheses. Alternatively, I would suggest that as this is the second time that the characters fight, "I, I" is a corruption of the roman numerals II to indicate a second round of the combat.

II.iv.95 late to fear] Dunstan, late, I fear.

II.iv.109 too fast] 1613, so fast.

Ch.II.10 weigh] 1613, way.

III.i.3 can make] 1613, cane mak.

III.i.26 bars] 1613, bares.

III.ii.6 filled] Purkiss 1994, fill.

III.ii.32 And her with you be ne'er the less] Dunstan, And here with you. Be ne'er the less; Cerasano and Wynne-Davies, And her with you, be near, the less.

III.ii.37 not] 1613, no.

III.ii.39 doom'd] 1613, done.

III.ii.41-42 I . . . our] 1613, he . . . his; Dunstan, Weller and Ferguson and Gutierrez, we . . . our; Purkiss 1994, I . . . his. The pronouns in the 1613 edition seem to make little sense, as Salome clearly wants Herod to think that she divorced Constabarus out of loyalty to him rather than a desire to marry Silleus. The "brother" of l.42 seems to refer to Herod.

III.ii.45 for told] Cerasano and Wynne-Davies, foretold.

III.ii.64 slight] 1613, slite; Weller and Ferguson, Purkiss 1994 and Gutierrez, sleight. Sleight or slight could be applicable in this context. There is likely to be a deliberate quibble on the two words as Salome uses both cunning and slander against Mariam. The Salome of *The Antiquities* is particularly given to slandering Mariamme.

III.ii.70 s.d. Enter Silleus' man] 1613, no s.d.

III.ii.81 bids] 1613, bides.

III.ii.86 s.d. Exeunt] 1613, no s.d.

III.iii.2 blue] 1613, blew.

III.iii.6 sp.n. Mariam] 1613, attributed to Sohemus.

III.iii.75 Alexandra's] 1613, Alexander's. "Alexandra's" would agree with that character's words at the end of I. ii, which imply that she and Mariam are currently ruling Judea. It would also agree with "her" in line 77.

III.iii.83 quit] 1613, quite.

III.iii.89 still, nay more, retorted] 1613, still. Nay more retorted; Cerasano and Wynne-Davies, still, nay, more retorted; Gutierrez, still. Nay more, retorted.

III.iii.96 s.d Exit] 1613, no s.d.
Ch.III.22 others, pray?] 1613, others pray?; Purkiss 1994, Weller and Ferguson, Gutierrez, others' prey?

IV.i.3 w'adore] Cerasano and Wynne-Davies, we adore.

IV.i.4 s.d Enter Nuntio] 1613, s.d. after line 5.

IV.i.5 my Mariam?] Dunstan, my Mariam, how?; Weller and Ferguson, my Mariam? How? This emendation, which gives a rhyme word for "brow," would require the contraction of Mariam to two syllables to retain the meter.

IV.i.16 Joshua-like] 1613, Josualike.

IV.i.24 grief] Dunstan, Purkiss 1994 and 1998, geese. Dunstan does not explain his suggested emendation, although his reading does correspond with the story of Marcus Manlius Capitolinus, the commander who held the Capitol against the Gauls at the sacking of Rome c. 390 BC. He is supposed to have been awakened by the cackling of geese while sleeping in his house on the Capitol – the dogs having failed to give a warning – and repulsed a surprise attack by the Gauls. Weller and Ferguson's gloss on "grief" (165), is sufficiently feasible to retain the original: "Rome would have been betrayed to the Volscians except for the grief which Coriolanus felt at the sight of his mother's pleading for the city's salvation," although Purkiss 1998 (188) disagrees.

IV.i.33 a little while, mine eyes] 1613, a little, while mine eyes.

IV.i.38 lest] 1613, least.

IV.i.39 s.d. Exit Nuntio] 1613, no s.d.

IV.ii. s.d Enter Pheroras] 1613, no s.d.

IV.ii.30 your will] 1613, you will.

IV.ii.37 Salome] 1613, Salom. The extra syllable has been inserted to retain the meter.

IV.ii.39 s.d. Exeunt Pheroras and attendants] 1613, no s.d.

IV.ii.42 Salome] 1613, Salom. The extra syllable has been inserted to retain the meter.

IV.ii.43 spirit] Cerasano and Wynne-Davies, sprite. Cerasano and Wynne-Davies emend to rhyme with "requite."

IV.ii.44 no s.d.] 1613, s.d. Exit.

IV.iii. s.d. Enter Mariam] 1613, no s.d.

IV.iii.42-44 Incomplete quatrain] Weller and Ferguson, Gutierrez and Purkiss 1998 place the missing line at the top of the quatrain.

IV.iv Enter Butler] 1613, no s.d.

IV.iv.6 poison] 1613, passion. With the exception of Gutierrez, all editors make this emendation. The scene shows the execution of Salome's plot as described in the Argument and III.ii 59-60, to convince Herod that Mariam means to poison him. This scene is directly lifted from Josephus (*Ant.*, 398).

IV.iv.14 s.d Exit Butler] 1613, no s.d. The s.d. "Enter Bu." appears later in the scene, indicating that the character must have made an exit at some point previously. This would seem to be the logical place, in order for the Butler to carry out Herod's command.

IV.iv.46 Yet never wert thou] Dunstan, Purkiss 1994, Cerasano and Wynne-Davies and Purkiss 1998, Yet wert thou; E MS, "never" underlined and a cross in the margin. The removal of "never" gives the line ten syllables.

IV.iv.53 nature-sullied ore] Purkiss 1994, Cerasano and Wynne-Davies and Gutierrez, nature sullied o'er.

IV.iv.56 heav'nly] 1613, heavy.

IV.iv.62 stars] 1613, stares.

IV.iv.70 guiltless] 1613, gulitles.

IV.iv.71 lock] 1613, looke.

IV.iv.75 s.d. Exit Butler] 1613, no s.d.

IV.iv.76 s.d. Enter Soldiers] 1613, no s.d.

IV.iv.81 bade] 1613, bad.

IV.iv.87 hath love] 1613, hath bove.

IV.iv.94 s.d. Exeunt Soldiers with Mariam] 1613, no s.d.

IV.iv.100 s.d. Exit] 1613, no s.d. Purkiss 1994, Cerasano and Wynne-Davies and Purkiss 1998 have Herod, Mariam and Soldiers all exiting here.

IV.v s.d. Enter Butler] 1613, no s.d.

IV.v.2 causeless] 1613, caules.

IV.v.19 didst not well] Dunstan and Cerasano and Wynne-Davies, didest well.

IV.vi.13 compliment] 1613, complement.

IV.vi.14 This] 1613, Tis; Dunstan, Thus.

IV.vi.20 our] 1613, your; A, our; Weller and Ferguson, Cerasano and Wynne-Davies and Gutierrez, her. The pronoun "your" does not appear to make any sense. Baba's sons have not been unlucky in marriage. Furthermore, Constabarus is trying to reassure them that they are not to blame for Salome's betrayal. Had Baba's sons been executed twelve years ago, as Herod ordered, it would not have prevented Salome and Constabarus' ill-fated marriage

IV.vi.23 Whereby] 1613, Were by; Wo MS, Where by.

IV.vi.26 duties. Friends should die] 1613, duties, friends should die; Purkiss 1994 and Cerasano and Wynne-Davies, duties: friends should die; Weller and Ferguson, duties; friends should die.

IV.vi.36 chase] Purkiss, chafe.

IV.vi.47 man] 1613, many.

IV.vi.54 wreck] 1613, wreack; Gutierrez, wreak.

IV.vi.58 she] 1613, he.

IV.vi.68 endued] 1613, indude; Purkiss 1994 and Weller and Ferguson, indued.

IV.vi.78 s.d. Exeunt] 1613, no s.d.

IV.vii.1 sp.n. Salome] 1613, First line attributed entirely to Herod. All other editors retain the 1613 format. However, "Die quoth you?" is apparently a question in response to Herod's first statement "Nay, she shall die." "That she shall!" is a confirmation in response to the question. It would seem reasonable to give "Die quoth you?" to Salome, who wants to make sure of Herod's state of mind before encouraging him to send the order for Mariam's execution. Bod.M has a MS caret between "die." and "Die," indicating an omission.

IV.vii.6 miracles] Dyce MS, merciless.

IV.vii.7 refell] Purkiss 1994, Gutierrez, and Purkiss 1998, repell.

IV.vii.12 fauchions] 1613, fanchions; Purkiss 1994, Weller and Ferguson and Cerasano and Wynne-Davies, falchions.

IV.vii.29 love be slain] A MS, life be pain.

IV.vii.33 Oh aye, I] 1613, Oh I: I.

IV.vii.33 s.d. Exit Salome] 1613, no s.d. The text demands that she exits and re-enters a short time later.

IV.vii.36 s.d. Enter Salome] 1613, no s.d.

IV.vii.44 Aye, very well.] 1613, I very well.

IV.vii.59 kings. The pride] 1613, Kings, the pride; Purkiss 1994, Weller and Ferguson and Cerasano and Wynne-Davies, kings; the pride.

IV.vii.60 Troy-flaming Helen's] Cerasano and Wynne-Davies, Troy's flaming Helen.

IV.vii.98 ebon-hewed] 1613, ebon-hewde; Bod.M, Weller and Ferguson, Purkiss 1994 and Cerasano and Wynne-Davies ebon-hued; Gutierrez, ebon-hew'd. The 1613 spelling has been emended to give the image of Mariam's eyes being sculpted from ebony, which fits with Herod's metaphor of Heaven as an artist creating Mariam as a self-portrait. Aurally, of course, either meaning can be deduced.

IV.vii.99 sable star] Cerasano and Wynne-Davies, stable star.
IV.vii.129 Asuerus] Cerasano and Wynne-Davies, Ahasuerus.

IV.vii.155 Ate] Purkiss 1994, ape.

IV.vii.168 s.d. Exit] 1613, no s.d.

IV.viii.3 Aye, I] 1613, I, I.

IV.viii.4 As] 1613, At.

IV.viii.15 sleights] 1613, slights.

IV.viii.51 In] 1613, I Weller and Ferguson and Cerasano and Wynne-Davies, Ay. Weller and Ferguson (172) claim that "'In heav'n' produces redundancy with 'thither'." However, Doris' exclamation could be a mocking repetition of Mariam's own words at the beginning of l.50.

IV.viii.68 babes for love] Cerasano and Wynne-Davies, babes? For love.

IV.viii.70 no stain did Doris' honour dim?] Cerasano and Wynne-Davies, no stain? Did Doris honour dim?

IV.viii.89 Gerarim] Dunstan and Weller and Ferguson, Gerizim; Cerasano and Wynne-Davies Gerazim.

Ch.IV.2 scorning] 1613, scorniug.

Ch.IV.12 wrestle] 1613, wrastle.

Ch.IV.35 proud] 1613, prou'd; Weller and Ferguson, Gutierrez, Purkiss 1998, prov'd; Cerasano and Wynne-Davies and Purkiss 1994, proved. Whilst the v/u substitution is feasible, proud gives the rhyme with allowed and also refers back to "virtuous pride" at the beginning of the line.
V.i.38 darken] 1613, darke; Gutierrez, dark.

V.i.55 sp.n. Herod] 1613, sp.n. Nuntio. All editors agree that the words should be attributed to Herod.

V.i.69 Were I not made her lord, I still should be] Dunstan, Weller and Ferguson and Cerasano and Wynne-Davies, Were I not mad, her lord I still should be. Although this is a feasible reading, the original problematises the term "lord." Herod is Mariam's "lord" in two senses, as her husband and her King. Herod's statement might then read "Were I not made her lord [in the sense of her King] I still should be [her lord in the sense of her husband]." A king could have his wife executed for adultery, a privilege not extended to his subjects.

V.i.80 divided] Dunstan, Purkiss 1994 and Cerasano and Wynne-Davies, divide.

V.i.85 died] 1613, did.

V.i.108 he] 1613, she.

V.i.137 'dressed] 1613, drest. The shortened version of "addressed" is appropriate as Herod is mildly castigating the Nuntio for his subordination in "pretending" to Herod that Mariam is dead.

V.i.190 died] 1613, did.

V.i.211 fame] Purkiss 1994, fain; Weller and Ferguson, Cerasano and Wynne-Davies and Gutierrez, feign; Purkiss 1998, faine.

V.i.213 fame] Purkiss 1994, fain; Weller and Ferguson, Cerasano and Wynne-Davies and Gutierrez, feign; Purkiss 1998, faine.

Ch.V.34 admirably] 1613, admirablie; Purkiss 1994 and Cerasano and Wynne-Davies, admirable.

Appendix A: Main Sources

[The main sources for *The Tragedy of Mariam* are *The Antiquities of the Jews* and *The Wars of the Jews*, originally written in Greek in the first century by Flavius Josephus. Both of these appeared in an English translation by Thomas Lodge entitled *The Famous and Memorable Works of Josephus*, 1602 (STC 14809). The extracts below are taken from this edition, copy-text from the Brotherton Library Special Collection, University of Leeds. Spelling and punctuation have been modernised, but no other substantive changes have been made to the original.]

1. *The Antiquities of the Jews*, Book XV, Chapter IIII, 387-88.
[A marginal note dates these events at 33-32 BC.]

[Alexandra] certified Cleopatra by her private letters of Herod's treasons, and her son's most miserable and untimely death. Cleopatra long before that time desirous to assist her, and having compassion of her misery, undertook the matter, and ceased not to incite Anthony to revenge Aristobolus' death, telling him that it was an unpardonable error, that Herod being created king in such a state, whereunto he had no right, should be suffered to practice such conspiracies against the true and lawful kings. Anthony persuaded by these her words (as soon as he came unto Laodicea) sent for Herod, to the end that making his appearance he might answer that which might be objected against him, as touching Aristobolus' death. For he disliked the act, notwithstanding that Herod himself had attempted it. But although Herod was afraid of this accusation, and did not a little suspect Cleopatra's displeasure (for that she ceased not continually to provoke Anthony against him) yet obeyed he this commandment, and transported himself thither (the rather for that he durst not otherwise do), notwithstanding he left his uncle Joseph behind him, committing the government both of the kingdom and his private estate unto him, giving him secret instructions to kill Mariamme, if so be that Anthony should happen to do him any mischief. For he loved her so extremely by reason of her beauty that he supposed himself injured, if after his decease she should be beloved by any other; and he openly declared that all that misery which befell him, proceeded from Anthony's passion and entire affection, and admiration of her beauty, whereof he had before time heard some report. As soon therefore as he had in this sort disposed his affairs, notwithstanding he had little hope of good hap, yet repaired he to Anthony.

But Joseph, governing that kingdom that was committed to his hands, conversed divers times upon this occasion with Mariamme, and communicated oftentimes with her, not only for public profit sake, but also to do her that honour which so great a princess deserved. At such time therefore as he secretly devised with her, as touching the friendship and ardent affection which Herod bore unto her, his speeches were jested at after the manner of ladies, but especially flouted at by Alexandra. For which cause Joseph, being over-forward to express the King's good will towards her, proceeded so far that he discovered the commandment that was given him, thereby to make manifest, that it was not possible for Herod to live without her, and that if any inconvenient should happen unto him, he would not in death also be disjoined from her. This discourse of Joseph's was not interpreted by the ladies as a demonstration of his good will, but rather as a manifestation of Herod's malignity, who dying, desired also that they should perish, and interpreted that which he had spoken as the testimony of his tyrannous and malicious heart. At that time there was a rumour spread in the city of Jerusalem by Herod's maligners, that Anthony had in such sort tormented him, that he was dead. Whereupon all those of the King's house were troubled, and in especial the ladies; so that Alexandra incited Joseph to forsake the palace, and take the ladies, and to retire himself under the ensigns of the Roman legion, who at that time were about the city for the security of the kingdom, under the conduct of the Tribune Julius, to the end first of all, that if any trouble should happen in the King's house, they might be by this means in safety, having the Romans to friend. And afterwards, for that they hoped that if Anthony should see Mariamme, she might obtain all things at his hands whatsoever she desired, assuring him that he would restore the kingdom unto her, and deprive her of nothing that concerned, or was answerable to, her royal estate.

But whilst they were distracted with these deliberations, there came letters from Herod, contrary to some few men's report, and all men's expectation. For as soon as he came unto Anthony, he compassed his favour by his many presents, which he had brought with him to that intent from Jerusalem, and suddenly debating the matter with him, he appeased him in such sort, as he was no more displeased against him; and from that time forward, Cleopatra's speeches were but coldly conceited of in regard of his so ample satisfaction. For Anthony said that there was no reason that a king should be answerable for that which he had done in his kingdom, for that in so doing he should no more be king, but that when the honour is once given him, he hath the authority likewise left him, to use his regal power; urging further, that it concerned Cleopatra likewise herself, not to search too curiously into the affairs and government of kingdoms. Herod certified all this by his letters, and signified further what other honours he had received at Anthony's hands in assemblies and feasts, to which he invited him always. Notwithstanding Cleopatra seemed to be displeased therewith, detracting him; and being desirous to get the kingdom of Jewry into her hands, strove by all means possible to put him to death: but that he had found Anthony always an upright man, and feared not henceforward that any evil should befall him, and returning presently upon this, he brought with him a more ample testimony of Anthony's most assured affection, both in respect of his own kingdom, as of his particular affairs. And as touching Cleopatra, she pretended not to seek any further than that which she had, because that Anthony had given her Coelesyria instead of that which she had demanded, forbearing thence forward to mention Jewry any more, because Anthony wholly rejected those suits.

After these letters came unto their hands, the trouble and disturbance wherein they were, and their desire to retire unto the Romans, as if Herod had been dead, was wholly extinguished. Yet was not this their resolution hidden from the King; but that Herod after he had brought Anthony on his way (who at that time set forward in his wars against the Parthians) he returned into Jewry. Upon his arrival, his sister Salome, and his mother certified him exactly of Alexandra's intent, and the determination of her friends. Salome likewise spake against Joseph her husband, and slandered him, objecting against him that he had had Mariamme's company. All which she spake thorow the malice she had long time conceived against him, for that in a certain debate Mariamme had in her rage despitefully hit them in the teeth with their obscure birth. Herod (who was always inflamed with the earnest affection which he bore unto his wife Mariamme) was suddenly troubled hereat: and although jealousy pressed him forward, yet love restrained him and kept him from doing anything rashly, thorow passion or affection. For which cause he called Mariamme aside and demanded of her in secret, what familiar company she had kept with Joseph? She by solemn oaths and by all possible allegations in her own defence appeased the King by little and little, and pacified his choler. For in such sort was he transported with the love that he bore unto his wife, that he believed she had sufficiently purged herself of those slanders that had been enforced against her; yielding her most hearty thanks for her honest affection towards him, and declaring unto her openly the great esteem and love that he bore unto her. Finally (as it often falleth out amongst lovers) they fell to tears, and embraced each other with great affection: and for that she gave him no credit, he endeavoured the more to draw her to belief. Whereupon Mariamme said unto him: "It is not the act of a lover to have given commandment, that if anything should befall thee otherways than well with Anthony, I should presently be done to death with thee; notwithstanding I have no ways offended thee." No sooner were these words out of her mouth, but the King entered into a strange passion, and giving over his embraces he cried out with a loud voice and tore his hair, saying, that he had a most evident proof that Joseph had committed adultery with her: for that he would not have discovered those things which had been spoken to him in secret, except they had greatly trusted the one the other. And in this emotion or rage of jealousy hardly contained he himself from killing his wife. But the force of love overcame him so much, that he bridled his rage, notwithstanding it were irksome and grievous unto him. Yet gave he order that Joseph should be slain without either audience or justification of his innocence; and as touching Alexandra, who was the cause of all these troubles, he kept her prisoner.

1a. *The Antiquities of the Jews*, Book XV, Chapter XI, 396-99.
[A marginal note dates these events at 29-28 BC.]

Mariamme . . . supposed that her husband did but dissemble his love, rather for his own profit and commodity, than for any entire affection he bore towards her. But nothing more grieved her, but that she had not any hope to live after him, if so be he should happen to die, especially for the order he had left as concerning her: neither could she ever forget what commandment before that time he had left with Joseph; so that by all means possible, she laboured to win the affections of those that had the charge of her; and especially Sohemus, knowing very well that her safety depended wholly on his hands, who in the beginning behaved himself very wisely and faithfully, containing himself very circumspectly within the bound of his commission. But after these ladies had with pretty presents and feminine flatteries mollified and wrought him by little and little, at last he blabbed out all that which the King had commanded him. Especially, for that he hoped not that he should return with the same power and authority which before he had: and for cause he thought thus in himself, that without incurring any danger in regard of Herod, he might greatly gratify the ladies; who in all likelihood should not be deprived of that dignity, wherein they were at that time; but would return him the like kindness when Mariamme should be Queen or next unto the King. Furthermore he hoped that if Herod also should return with all things answerable to his desires, that he would perform nothing without his wife's consent; or upbraid him with the act, if she contradicted. For he knew too well that the King loved her in such sort, as it was impossible to equal or express his affections; and for these causes he disclosed the trust that was committed unto him. But Mariamme was very sore displeased to hear that there was no end of her miseries, but that they were altogether united and tied to the dangers of Herod; and she oftentimes wished that he might never more return again in safety, supposing that her life with him should be very intolerable, all which she afterwards dissembled not, but openly confessed that which afflicted her with discontent. For whenas Herod beyond all expectation arrived in his country, being adorned with mighty fortune, he first of all, as it became him, certified his wife of his good tidings and happy success, whom only amongst all other his friends and wives, he embraced and saluted, for the pleasing conversation and affection that was in her. But she, whilst he repeated unto her these fortunate events of his affairs, rather entertained the same with a displeasant attention, than applauding joy; and these affections of hers like-wise she could not conceal. For at such time as he folded his arms about her neck, she unfolded her sorrow in her sighs; so simple and unfeigned were her affections; and seemed rather to be displeased that appeased by his narrations. Whereupon Herod was sore troubled, perceiving these things not only suspected, but also fully manifest. But above all things he was distracted when he considered the incredible and apparent hatred that his wife had conceived against him; which in such sort incensed him that he could not resist the love that had attainted him; so that he neither could continue in wrath, nor listen long to peace. And being unresolved in himself, he now was attempted by this; straight distracted by a contrary affection, so much was his mind travailed between love and hatred, that whenas oftentimes he desired to punish the woman's pride, his heart by love's mediation failed him in the enterprise. For nothing did more torment him than this fear, lest executing his displeasure against her, he should by this means more grievously wound himself, thorow the desire he bore unto his deceased delight. Whilst thus he was sweltered and devoured in his passions, and conceived sinister opinions against Mariamme his wife, Salome his sister and his mother having an inkling of his discontents, thought that they had gotten a fit opportunity to express and execute their hatred towards Mariamme. For which cause they conferred with Herod, and whetted his spleen and displeasure with variety of slanders, sufficient at one assault to engender hatred, and kindle his jealousy against her. To these reproaches of theirs, he lent no unwilling ears; yet had he not the heart to attempt anything against his wife, or to give free credit to their report, notwithstanding his displeasure increased, and was inflamed more and more against her, for that neither she could colour her cares and discontents, nor he contain himself from exchanging his love into hatred. And perhaps at that time he had published some fatal doom against her, had not a happy messenger brought him word, that Anthony and Cleopatra being dead, Caesar was become Lord of Egypt: for which cause hasting forward to meet and entertain him, he left his family in that present estate. Upon his departure he recommended Mariamme to Sohemus giving him great thanks for the care he had had of her, and granted him in way of gratuity a part of Jewry to govern.

When Herod was arrived in Egypt, and had friendly and familiarly conferred with Caesar, he was highly honoured by him: for Caesar gave him those four hundred Frenchmen that were of Cleopatra's guard, and restored that part of his country unto him again, which was taken away and spoiled by her. He annexed also unto his kingdom Gadara, Hippon, and Samaria, and on the sea coasts the cities of Gaza, Anthedon, Ioppe, with the tower of Straton: which when he had obtained, he grew more mighty than before. And after he had accompanied Caesar as far as Antioch, he returned into his own country. Upon his arrival, he found that fortune which was favourable unto him abroad, too froward at home, especially in regard of his wife, in whose affection before time he seemed to be most happy. For he was as inwardly touched with the lawful love of Mariamme, as any other of whom the Histories make report. And as touching her, she was both chaste and faithful unto him. Yet had she a certain womanly imperfection and natural forwardness, which was the cause that she presumed too much upon the entire affection wherewith her husband was entangled; so that without regard of his person, who had power and authority over others, she entertained him oftentimes very outrageously. All which he endured patiently, without any show of discontent. But Mariamme upbraided and publicly reproached both the King's mother and sister, telling them that they were but abjectly and basely born. Whereupon there grew a great enmity and unrecoverable hatred between the ladies; and from thence also there arose an occasion of greater accusations and calumnations than before. These suspicions were nourished amongst them, for the space of one whole year after Herod's return from Caesar; and finally this long contrived, and fore-imagined hatred at last broke out violently upon this occasion that ensueth. Whenas about midday the King had withdrawn himself into his chamber to take his rest, he called Mariamme unto him to sport with her, being incited thereunto by the great affection that he bore unto her. Upon this his command she came in unto him; yet would she not lie with him, nor entertain his courtings with friendly acceptance, but upbraided him bitterly with her father's and brother's death. The King took these reproachful words in very evil part, and was almost ready to strike her, but his sister hearing a greater stir and noise within than was usual, sent in the butler, who long before that time was suborned by her, whom she commanded to tell the King that Mariamme had prepared a drink for him to incite and quicken him unto love, willing him that if the King should be moved thereat, and should demand what he meant, he should certify him, that Mariamme having prepared a poison for his grace, had dealt with him to deliver it to his Majesty. Charging him moreover, that if the King, in hearing him speak of this potion, should seem to be moved therewith, that then he should proceed no further in his discourse. He therefore (being in this manner before hand instructed what he ought to do) at that very instant was sent in to discover his treachery unto the King. For which cause with a sober and staid countenance he entered in unto him, being seriously and well prepared to discourse, and told him that Mariamme had bribed him to present his Majesty with an amorous cup of drink. Now when he perceived that the King was troubled with these words, he prosecuted his discourse, alleging that the potion was a certain medicine which Mariamme had given him, the virtue whereof he knew not, which he had received according as he had told him, knowing that it concerned both his own security, and the King's safety.

Herod, who before this was highly displeased, hearing these words, was so much the more incensed, for which cause he presently commanded Mariamme's most faithful servant to be examined by torments, as concerning the poison, supposing that it was impossible for her to undertake anything whatsoever, without his privity. He being tired and tormented after this cruel manner, confessed nothing of that for which he was tortured, but declared unto the King that the hatred which his wife had conceived against him, proceeded from certain words that Sohemus had told her. Scarcely had he finished these words, but that the King cried out with a loud voice, saying, that Sohemus, who before time had been most faithful both to him and his kingdom, would not have declared these his privy commands, except there had been some more inward familiarity and secrecy betwixt him and Mariamme, for which cause he presently commanded his ministers to lay hands on Sohemus, and to put him to death. As for his wife, he drew her to her trial, and to this effect he assembled his most familiar friends, before whom he began to accuse her with great spite and spleen, as touching these potions and poisons aforesaid; wherein he used intemperate and unseemly speeches, and such as for their bitterness did ill become him in cause of justice. So that in the end the assistants, seeing the butt and bent of his desire, pronounced sentence of death against her: which being passed, both he, and all other the assistants were of this opinion, that she should not so speedily be executed, but that she should be kept close prisoner in some sure place of the palace. But by Salome's solicitations Herod was incited to hasten her death, for that she alleged that the King ought to fear, lest some sedition should be raised amongst the people, if he should keep her alive in prison. And by this means Mariamme was led unto her death.

Alexandra, her mother, considering the estate of the time, and fearing no less mischief from Herod's hands, than her daughter was assured of, she undecently changed her mind, and abjectedly laid aside her former courage, and magnanimity. For intending to make it known, that she was neither party nor privy to those crimes wherewith Mariamme was charged, she went out to meet her daughter, and entertained her injuriously, protesting publicly that she was a wicked woman, and ungrateful towards her husband, and that she well deserved the punishment that was adjudged her, for that she durst be so bold to attempt so heinous a fact, neglecting to requite her husband's entire love, with her unfeigned loyalty. Whilst thus dishonestly she counterfeited her displeasure, and was ready to pull Mariamme by the hair, the assistants, according to her desert, condemned her generally for her shameful hypocrisy. But she that was led to be punished, convicted her by her mild behaviour. For first of all, she gave her no answer, neither was any ways altered by her reproaches, neither would so much as cast her eye upon her; making it appear that she discreetly concealed and covered her mother's imperfections, and was aggrieved that she had so openly showed so great indignity: expressing for her own part a constant behaviour; and going to her death without change of colour, so that those that beheld her, perceived in her a kind of manifest courage and nobility, even in her utmost extremity. Thus died Mariamme, having been a woman that excelled both in continence and courage, notwithstanding that she defaulted somewhat in affability and impatience of nature. For the rest of her parts, she was of an admirable and pleasing beauty, and of such carriage in those companies wherein she was entertained, that it was impossible to express the same, in that she surpassed all those of her time, which was the principal cause that she lived not graciously and contentedly with the King. For being entertained by him, who entirely loved her, and from whom she received nothing that might discontent her, she presumed upon a great and intemperate liberty in her discourse. She digested also the loss of her friends very hardly, according as in open terms she made it known unto the King, whereby also it came to pass, that both Herod's mother, and sister, and himself likewise grew at odds with her, and in especial her husband, from whom only she expected no hard measure.

After her death the King began more powerfully to be inflamed in his affections, who before times, as we have declared, was already miserably distracted. For neither did he love after the common manner of married folk, but whereas almost even unto madness he nourished this his desire. He could not be induced by the too unbridled manners of his wife to allay the heat of his affections, but that daily more and more by doting on her, he increased the same. And all that time especially he supposed that God was displeased with him, for the death of Mariamme his wife. Oftentimes did he invoke her name, and more often undecently lamented he her. And notwithstanding he devised all kind of delights and sports that might be imagined, by preparing banquets, and inviting guests with princely hospitality, to pass away the time; yet all those profited him nothing. For which cause he gave over the charge and administration of his kingdom. And in such sort was he overwhelmed with grief, that oftentimes he commanded his ministers to call his wife Mariamme, as if she had yet been alive. Whilst thus he was affected, there befell a pestilence within the city, that consumed a great sort of the people, and the better part of the nobility, and each man interpreted that this punishment was inflicted by God upon men, for the unjust death of the Queen. Thus the King's discontents being by these means increased, he at last hid himself in a solitary wilderness under pretext of hunting, where afflicting himself incessantly, at last he fell into a most grievous sickness. This disease of his was an inflammation or pain in the neck; he seemed also in some sort to rave and wax mad. Neither could any remedies relieve him of his agony, but whenas the sickness seemed rather to increase, all men at last grew almost desperate of his recovery. For which cause his physician, partly in respect of the contumacy of his disease, partly, because in so great danger there was not any free election of diet, they gave him leave to taste whatsoever best pleased his appetite, committing the uncertain event of his health to the hands of fortune.

1b. *The Antiquities of the Jews,* Book XV, Chapter XI, 400-01.
[A marginal note dates these events at 28 BC.]

Costabarus was an Idumean, and one of the greatest account amongst his countrymen, who was descended from the Priests of Cozas, whom the Idumeans esteem for a God. Now after that Hircanus had drawn the policy of the Idumeans to the reformed customs of the Jews, Herod was made King of the Jews, and appointed Costabarus to be governor in Idumea and Gaza, giving him Salome his sister to wife, after he had put Joseph to death, to whom she had been married before time, as we have heretofore declared. Costabarus seeing himself in this estate beyond his expectation, grew more elate and proud than his good fortune required, and in a little time forgot himself so far, that he thought himself dishonoured, if he should perform that which Herod commanded him, and scorned that the Idumeans should be under the Jews subjection, notwithstanding they had received their manner of government from them. He therefore sent messengers unto Cleopatra, giving her to understand that Idumea had always been under her ancestors' subjection, and for that cause she ought upon just cause to demand and beg that country at Antonius' hands, and that in respect of himself he was ready to become her servant. All which he practiced, not to gratify Cleopatra in any sort whatsoever, but to the intent that if Herod's fortunes should be any ways weakened, he might more easily by this means both enlarge and obtain the kingdom of Idumea. And with these foolish hopes was he transported in regard of his birth and riches, which he had heaped together, by such dishonest means, as he continually practiced as he that intended no small matters. But notwithstanding Cleopatra's often and earnest petition to obtain this sovereignty, yet could she not obtain it at Antonius' hands. When Herod had notice of these covert and cunning practices, he was ready to kill Costabarus, but upon the earnest supplications of his sister and her mother, he dismissed and pardoned him, yet held him always in suspicion, by reason of this his practice. Not long after, it happened, that Salome fell at debate with Costabarus, for which cause she sent a libel of divorce to her husband, notwithstanding it were against the laws and ordinary customs of the Jews. For according to our ordinances, it is only lawful for the husband to do the same and as touching the wife, notwithstanding she were separated, yet is it not lawful for her to marry again, except her husband first give her license. But Salome without respect of the laws of the country, grounding herself too much upon her own authority, forsook her husband, saying, that she separated herself from her husband, by reason of the great friendship which she bore unto her brother, for that she had received some notice that Costabarus practiced some innovation with Antipater, Lysimachus and Dositheus. And this accusation of hers confirmed she by Baba's children, whom he had already kept with him in all security for the space of twelve years. All which was true, and at that time beyond all men's expectation wonderfully troubled Herod, as soon as he heard it. For as touching Baba's sons, he had heretofore resolved to cut them off, for that they had been always badly affected towards him and all his enterprises, but all that time he had let them pass, because by continuance they were grown out of his remembrance. Now the cause of this enmity and hatred which he bore towards them, was gathered from this ground. At such time as Antigonus enjoyed the sovereignty, and Herod beseiged the city of Jerusalem with an army; now those incommodities and necessities that ordinarily happen unto those that are besieged, were the cause that divers acknowledged Herod, and fixed their hopes upon him. But Baba's sons being in authority, and besides that, attended by a great number of men, persevered in their faithful observation of Antigonus, and blamed Herod continually, encouraging the inhabitants to continue the kingdom in those to whom it appertained by descent, and they themselves followed that course, which in their opinion was most profitably for the commonwealth. But after that the city was surprised by Herod, and he grew master of the estate, Costabarus, who was appointed to keep the city gates, and to lie in wait that none of those who were accused to have forsaken the King's side, should escape, knowing that the sons of Baba were greatly esteemed and honoured among the people, and foreseeing that their safety might be no small furtherance to himself, if at any time there might befortune any alteration; he discharged, and hid them within own possessions. And notwithstanding that at that time he had protested to Herod by an oath, that he knew not was become of them, yet, though suspected of perjury, he concealed them. And afterwards when the King had by proclamation promised a reward to him that should discover them, and sought for them by all means, neither then also would he confess the fact. For being afraid lest he should be punished for his first denial, he continued thorow concealment, being not only now driven thereunto by friendship but also by necessity.

1c. *The Antiquities of the Jews.* Book XVI, Chapter XI, 425.
[A marginal note dates these events at 7 BC.]

. . . the King's wives wished evil unto [Salome], because they knew her to be of strange qualities and hard to please, and so variable, that according to the time, one while she would profess friendship, and presently after hatred. Wherefore they still had something to inform Herod of against her, taking occasion happening by chance, which was this. There was a king of the Arabians, named Obodas, a slothful man, and one given to idleness; and there was one Syllaeus that did govern all his affairs. This man was a crafty fellow, and in the prime of his youth, and very beautiful. This Syllaeus coming unto Herod about some business, and viewing Salome, who then sat at supper with him, began to set his mind upon her, and finding she was a widow, he entered into talk with her, and she finding her brother now not so friendly unto her as before he had been, and also entangled with the beauty of this young man, did not greatly deny to marry him, and many feasts being made at that time, they showed evident signs of their mutual consent, and love one unto another. The King's wives told King of this in scoffing sort. Herod herewith nor contented, demanded of Pheroras how the matter stood, and willed him at supper time to note if he could espy any tokens of familiarity betwixt them. And Pheroras told him that by signs and mutual viewing one another, they sufficiently showed their intents. After this, the Arabian being suspected, departed into his own country. But two or three months after he came again into Judea, only for this purpose, and talked with Herod concerning this matter, requesting him to let Salome be his wife, affirming that that affinity would be profitable unto him for the traffic between his people and the Arabians, whose prince he was to be, and did already enjoy a great part of the dominion. Herod told all this unto his sister, and asked her if she would marry him: and she answered, she would. Then they requested that Syllaeus should become a Jew in religion, or else it was not lawful for him to marry her. He would nor condescend hereunto, affirming that he should be stoned to death by his people, if he did it; and so he departed without obtaining his purpose. From that time forth, Pheroras, and especially the King's wives accused Salome of intemperancy, affirming that she had had the company of the Arabian.

2. *The Wars of the Jews*, Book I, Chapter XVII, 589-90.

But his private and domestical sorrows seemed to envy him his public felicity, and most adverse fortune befell him through the means of a woman, whom he loved as himself. For being now made King, he put away his wife, which he first married (which was a lady born in Jerusalem, whose name was Doris) and married Mariamme the daughter of Alexander, who was Aristobolus' son, which caused troubles in his house, both before, but especially after he returned from Rome. For he banished his eldest son Antipater, whom he had by Doris, out of the city, only for his children's sake that he had by Mariamme, licensing him only at festival times to come unto the city in regard of some suspicion of treason intended against him. And afterward he slew Hyrcanus his wife's uncle, notwithstanding he returned out of Parthia unto him, because after he suspected that he intended some treason against him; whom Barzapharnes, after he had taken all Syria, took away prisoner with him. But his own countrymen that dwelt beyond Euphrates in commiseration redeemed him from thraldom and had he been counselled by them and not come unto Herod, he had not been killed. But the marriage of his niece caused his death; for, for that cause, and especially for the love of his native soil, he came thither. That which moved Herod to kill him was, not for that he sought the kingdom, but because he had right unto the kingdom. Herod had five children by Mariamme, two daughters and three sons. The youngest was sent unto Rome to study, where he died. The other two he brought up like princes both for their mother's nobility sake, and for that they were born after he was King. But that which above all other was most forcible, was the love he bore unto Mariamme, which from day to day tormented him more violently in such sort, that he felt not any part of those griefs which this his best beloved enforced against him. For Mariamme hated him as much as he loved her, and having a just cause and colour of discontent, moreover being emboldened by the love which he bore her, she every day upbraided him with that which he had done unto Hyrcanus her uncle, and unto her brother Aristobolus. For Herod spared him not although, he was a child, but after he had made him High Priest in the seventeenth year of his age, he presently put him to death after he had so honoured him, who when he came to the altar clothed in the sacred attire upon a festival day, all the people wept, and the same night he was sent into Jericho and drowned in like by the Galatheans, who had received commission to perform the murder. These things did Mariamme daily cast in Herod's teeth, and upbraided both his mother and sister, with very sharp reproachful words: yet he so loved her, that notwithstanding all this he held his peace. But the women were set on fire, and that they might the rather move Herod against her, they accused her of adultery, and of many other things which bore a show of truth, objecting against her that she had sent her portraiture into Egypt unto Antonius; and that through immoderate lust, she did what she could to make herself known unto him, who doted upon women's love, and was of sufficient power to do what wrong he pleased.

Hereat Herod was sore moved, especially for that he was jealous of her whom he loved, bethinking himself upon the cruelty of Cleopatra, for whose sake King Lysania and Malichus, King of

Arabia were put to death. And now he measured not the danger by the loss of his wife, but by his own death which he feared: for which cause being drawn by his affairs into the country, he gave secret commandment unto Joseph, his sister Salome's husband (whom he knew to be trusty, and one who for affinity was his well wisher) to kill his wife Mariamme, if so be Antonius should have killed him. But Joseph, not maliciously, but simply to show her how greatly the King loved her, disclosed that secret unto her; and she when Herod was returned, and amongst other talk with many oaths swore that he never loved woman but her. "Indeed" (quoth she) "it may be well known how greatly you love me by the commandment you gave to Joseph, whom you charged to kill me." Herod hearing this which he thought to be secret, was like a madman, and presently persuaded himself Joseph would never have disclosed that commandment of his, except he had abused her. So that hereupon he became furious, and leaping out of his bed, he walked up and down the palace: whereupon his sister Salome having fit opportunity, confirmed his suspicion of Joseph. For which cause Herod growing now raging mad with jealousy commanded both of them to be killed. Which done, his wrath was seconded by repentance and after his anger ceased, the affection of love was presently renewed. Yea, so great was the power of his affection that he would not believe she was dead, but spake unto her as though she was alive, until in process of time being ascertained of her funeral, he equalled the affection he bore her during her life, by the vehemence of his passion for her death.

2a. *The Wars of the Jews*, Book I, Chapter XVII, 592-93.

[Pheroras] was fellow with his brother of all, saving only the crown, and had his own revenues amounting to a hundred talents a year, and received all fruits of the whole country beyond Jordan, which was given him by his brother. Herod also obtained of Caesar to make him Tetrarch, and bestowed upon him a princess for his wife, despousing unto him his wife's sister, after whose decease he despoused unto him his eldest daughter and gave him three hundred talents with her for a dowry. But Pheroras fell in love with his maid, and forsook a princess; whereat Herod being angry married his daughter unto his brother's son, who was afterward slain by the Parthians; but Herod presently pardoned Pheroras' offence. Divers before this time were of the opinion that in the lifetime of the Queen [i.e., Mariam] he would have poisoned Herod. And Herod although he loved his brother very well, yet because many had access unto him told him so, he began to misdoubt: and so examining many that were suspected, lastly he came to Pheroras' friends, and none of them confessed it. Yet they confessed that he was determined to fly unto the Parthians with her whom he was so in love withal, and that Costabarus, Salome's husband was privy thereunto, unto whom the King married her after her first husband for suspicion of adultery was put to death. Salome herself also was not free from accusation, for Pheroras accused her that she had contracted matrimony with Syllaeus, who was procurator to Oboda, King Arabia, who was a great enemy of the King's, and she being convicted both of this and all things else, whereof her brother Pheroras accused her, yet obtained pardon, as likewise Pheroras did[.]

Appendix B: Selected Didactic and Polemical Texts

[What follows is a collection of extracts from didactic and polemical texts published in the sixteenth and early seventeenth centuries. The extracts have been selected to demonstrate the ways in which Church, State and household were conceived of and described in similar ways, with a particular focus upon the role and position of women within these institutions. The extracts have been arranged in order of publication of the copy-text. All copy-texts are from the UMI microfilm series Early English Books 1475-1640. Spelling and punctuation have been modernised, but no other substantive changes have been made to the original. Biblical references are given in square brackets in the main body of the text.]

I. Juan Luis Vives, *A very fruitful and pleasant book called the Instruction of a Christian Woman*, trans. Richard Hyrde, 1540 (STC 24856), sigs. E2^r-E3^r.
From "Of the Learning of Maids."

When she shall be taught to read, let those books be taken in hand, that may teach good manners. And when she shall learn to write, let not her example be void verses, nor wanton or trifling songs, but some sad sentence, prudent and chaste, taken out of holy scripture, or the sayings of philosophers, which by often writing she may fasten better in her memory. And in learning, as I point none end to the man, no more I do to the woman; saving it is meet that the man have knowledge of many and divers things, that may both profit himself and the commonwealth, both with the use and increasing of learning. But I would the woman should be altogether in that part of philosophy, that taketh upon it to inform, and teach and amend the conditions. Finally let her learn for herself alone and her young children, or her sisters in our Lord. For it neither becometh a woman to rule a school, nor to live among men, or speak abroad, and shake off her demureness and honesty, either all together or else a great part: which if she be good it were better to be at home within and unknown to other folks. And in company to hold her tongue demurely. And let few see her, and none at all hear her. The apostle Paul, the vessel of election, informing and teaching the church of the Corinthis with holy precepts, saith: Let your women hold their tongues in congregations: nor they be not allowed to speak but to be subject as the law biddeth. If they would learn anything, let them ask their husbands at home [1 Cor. 14:34-35]. And unto his disciple Timothy he writeth on this wise: Let a woman learn in silence with all subjection. But I give no license to a woman to be a teacher, nor to have authority of the man, but to be in silence. For Adam was the first made, and after Eve, and Adam was not betrayed, the woman was betrayed in to the breach of the commandment [1 Tim. 2:11-14]. Therefore, because a woman is a frail thing, and of weak discretion, and that may lightly be deceived; which thing our first mother Eve showeth, whom the devil caught with a light argument. Therefore a woman should not teach, lest when she hath taken a false opinion and believe of anything, she spread it into the hearers by the authority of mastership, and lightly bring others into the same error, for the learners commonly do after the teacher with a good will.

2. *The second tome of homilies, of such matters as were provided and entitled in the former part of homilies, set out by the authority of the Queen's Majesty. And to be read in every parish Church agreeably*, 1563 (STC 13651), sigs Tttt^V-Tttt2^r; Tttt3^r-Tttt4^r; Tttt4^V-Uuuu^V. From "The Sermon of the state of Matrimony."

The word of Almighty God doth testify and declare, whence the original beginning of matrimony cometh, and why it is ordained. It is instituted of God, to the intent that man and woman should live lawfully in a perpetual friendly fellowship, to bring forth fruit, and to avoid fornication, by which means, a good conscience might be preserved on both parties, in bridling the corrupt inclinations of the flesh, within the limits of honesty. For God hath straightly forbidden all whoredom and uncleanness, and hath from time to time taken grievous punishments of this inordinate lust, as all stories and ages hath declared. Furthermore, it is also ordained that the Church of God and his kingdom might, by this kind of life, be conserved and enlarged, not only in that God giveth children by his blessing, but also in that they be brought up by the parents godly, in the knowledge of God's word, that this the knowledge of God and true religion, might be delivered by the succession from one to another, that finally, many might enjoy that everlasting immortality. Wherefore, forasmuch as matrimony serveth as well to avoid sin and offence as to increase the kingdom of God, you, as all other which enter that state, must acknowledge this benefit of God, with pure and thankful minds, for that he hath so ruled your hearts, that ye follow not the example of the wicked world, who set their delight in filthiness of sin, where both of you stand in the fear of God, and abhor all filthiness. . . .

Learn thou therefore, if thou desirest to be void of all these miseries, if thou desirest to live peaceably and comfortably in wedlock, how to make thy earnest prayer to God, that he would govern both your hearts by his holy spirit, to restrain the devil's power, whereby your concord may remain perpetually. But to this prayer, must be joined a singular diligence, whereof St. Peter giveth his precept saying: You husbands deal with your wives according to knowledge, giving honour to the wife, as unto the weaker vessel, and as unto them that are heirs also of the grace of life, that your prayers be not hindered [1 Peter 3:7]. This precept doth peculiarly pertain to the husband. For he ought to be the leader and author of love, in cherishing and increasing concord, which then shall take place if he will use measurableness and not tyranny, and if he yield some things to the woman. For the woman is a weak creature, not endued with like strength and constancy of mind, therefore they be the sooner disquieted, and they be the more prone to all weak affections and dispositions of mind, more than men be, and lighter they be, and more vain in their fantasies and opinions. These things must be considered of the man, that he be not too stiff, so that he ought to wink at some things, and must gently expound all things, and to forbear. Howbeit, the common sort of men doth judge, that such moderation should not become a man. For they say, that it is a token of womanish cowardness, and therefore they think that it is a man's part to fume in anger, to fight with fist and staff. Howbeit, howsoever they imagine, undoubtedly St. Peter doth better judge what should be seeming to a man, and what he should most reasonably perform. For he saith, reasoning should be used, and not fighting. Yea he saith more, that the woman ought to have a certain honour attributed to her, that is to say, she must be spared and borne with, the rather for that she is the weaker vessel, of a frail heart, inconstant and, with a word, soon stirred to wrath. And therefore considering these her frailties, she is to be the rather spared. By this means, thou shalt not only nourish concord, but shalt have her heart in thy power and will. For honest natures will sooner be retained to do their duty, rather by gentle words, than by stripes. But he which will do all things with extremity and severity, and doth use always rigour in words, and stripes, what will that avail in the conclusion? Merely nothing, but that he thereby setteth forward the devil's work, he banisheth away concord, charity, and sweet amity, and bringeth in dissension, hatred, and irksomness, the greatest griefs that can be in the mutual love and fellowship of man's life. . . .

Now as concerning the wife's duty, what shall become her? Shall she abuse the gentleness and humanity of her husband? And at her pleasure turn all things upside down? No, surely, for that is far repugnant against God's commandment. For thus does St. Peter preach to them: Ye wives be ye in subjection to obey your own husband [1 Peter 3:1]. To obey is another thing than to control or command, which they may do to their children and to their family. But as for their husbands, them must they obey, and cease from commanding, and perform subjection. For this surely doth nourish concord very much, when the wife is ready at hand at her husband's commandment, when she will apply herself to his will, when she endeavoureth herself to seek his contentation, and to do him pleasure, when she will eschew all things that might offend him. For thus will most truly be verified by the saying of the Poet: A good wife by obeying her husband, shall bear the rule, so that he shall have a delight and a gladness, the sooner at all times to return home to her. But on the contrary part, when the wives be stubborn, froward, and malapert, their husbands are compelled thereby to abhor and flee from their own houses, even as they should have battle with their enemies. Howbeit, it can scantly be, but that some offences shall sometime chance betwixt them. For no man doth live without fault, specially for that the women is the more frail part. Therefore let them beware that they stand not in their faults and wilfulness, but rather let them acknowledge their follies, and say: My husband, so it is, that by my anger I was compelled to do this or that, forgive it me, I hereafter will take better heed. Thus ought women the more readily to do, the more they be ready to offend. And they shall not do this only to avoid strife and debate: but rather in the respect of the commandment of God, as St. Paul expresseth it in this form of words: Let women be subject to their husbands as to the Lord. For the husband is the head of the woman, as Christ is the head of the Church [Ephes.5:22-23].

3. Robert Cleaver, *A godly form of household government: for the ordering of private families, according to the direction of God's word,* 1598 (STC 5387), 1; 189-92; 220-22.

A household, is as it were, a little commonwealth, by the good government whereof, God's glory may be advanced, the commonwealth which standeth of several families benefitted, and all that live in that family may receive much comfort and commodity. . . .

In the days of Moses, husbands were easily and soon entreated to forsake their wives, by giving them a Bill of divorce: yet so far was this course from being lawful, that contrariwise, Jesus Christ saith that it was tolerated only in respect of the hardness of husband's hearts, who otherwise would have vexed their wives, and entreated them cruelly [Math.19:8].

And this libel, containing the cause of divorce, and putting away of the woman, did justify her, and condemn the man. For seeing it was never given in case of adultery (which was punished with death [Levit. 20:10, John 8:5]) all other causes alleged in the libel, tended to justify the woman, and declare, that she was wrongfully divorced, and so condemn the husband, as one that contraried the first institution of marriage. Whereto Jesus Christ condemning this corruption, doth return the saying: It was not so from the beginning, and therefore whosoever shall put away his wife, except it be for whoredom, and marrieth another, commit adultery: and whosoever marrieth her, which is divorced, doth commit adultery with her [Math.19:7-9]. So straight is the bond of marriage.

Hereof it followeth, that notwithstanding, whatsoever difficulties, that may arise between the husband and the wife, whether it be long, tedious, and incurable sickness of either party; whether natural and contrary humours, that breed debate, wrangling, or strife, about household affairs; whether it be any vice, as the husband to be a drunkard, or the wife a slothful, idle or unthrifty huswife; whether either party forsake the truth, and profession of religion, do fall to idolatry or heresy. Yet still the bond of marriage remaineth steadfast, and not to be dissolved. Neither may they be separated, even by their own mutual consent. For as the holy Ghost that pronounced: That which God hath joined together, let no man put asunder [Math.19:6]. . . .

As the Church should depend upon the wisdom, discretion and will of Christ, and not follow what itself listeth, so must the wife also submit and apply herself to the discretion and will of her husband, even as the government and conduct of everything resteth in the head, not in the body [Ephes. 5:22-24]. Moses writeth that the serpent was wise above all beasts of the field [Gen. 3:1], and that he did declare in assaulting the woman, that when he had seduced her, she might also seduce and deceive her husband. St. Paul noting this, among other the causes of the woman's subjection, doth sufficiently show, that for the avoiding of the like inconveniences, it is God's will, that she should be subject to her husband, so that she shall have no other discretion or will, but what may depend upon her head [1 Tim. 2:14]. As also the same Moses saith: Thy desire shall be subject to thy husband and he shall rule over thee [Gen. 3:16]. This dominion over the wife's will doth manifestly appear in this, that God in old time ordained, that if the woman had vowed anything unto God [Num. 30:7], it should notwithstanding rest in her husband to disavow it.

So much is the wife's will subject to her husband, yet is it not meant, that the wife should not employ her knowledge and discretion, which God hath given her, in the help and for the good of her husband. But always as it must be with condition to submit herself unto him, acknowledging him to be her head, that finally they may agree in one, as the conjunction of marriage doth require. Yet as when in a Lute, or other musical instrument, two strings concurring in one tune, the sound nevertheless is imputed to the strongest and highest, so in a well ordered household, there must be a communication, and consent of counsel and will, between the husband and the wife, yet such, as the counsel and commandment may rest in the husband.

True it is, that some women are wiser and more discreet than their husbands. As Abigall the wife of Naball, and others. Whereupon Solomon saith: A wise woman buildeth up the house, and blessed is the man, that hath a discreet wife [Prov. 14:1, 19:14, 31:10]. Yet still a great part of the discretion of such women, shall rest in acknowledging their husbands to be their heads, and so using the graces that they have received of the Lord, that their husbands may be honoured, not contemned, neither of them, nor of others, which falleth out contrary, when the wife will seem wiser than her husband.

So that this modesty and government ought to be in a wife: namely, that she should not speak but to her husband, or by her husband. And as the voice of him that soundeth a trumpet, is not so loud as the sound it yieldeth: so is the wisdom and word of a woman, of greater virtue and efficacy, when all that she knoweth, and can do, is, as if it were said and done by her husband.

4. *The Book of Common Prayer and Administration of the Sacraments, and other Rites and Ceremonies of the Church of England,* 1603 (STC 16326), sigs. P2ʳ-P3ʳ.
From "The Form of the Solemnisation of Matrimony."

All ye which be married, or which intend to take the holy estate of Matrimony upon you, hear what holy Scripture doth say as touching the duty of husbands towards their wives, and wives towards their husbands.

St. Paul, in his Epistle to the Ephesians, the fifth Chapter, doth give this commandment to all married men: Ye husbands, love your wives, even as Christ loved the Church, and hath given himself for it, to sanctify it, purging it in the fountain of water, through the Word, that he might make it unto himself a glorious congregation, not having spot or wrinkle, or any such thing, but that it should be holy and blameless. So men are bound to love their wives, as their own bodies. He that loveth his own wife, loveth himself, for never did any man hate his own flesh, but nourisheth and cherisheth it, even as the Lord doth the congregation. For we are members of his body, of his flesh, and of his bones. For this cause shall a man leave his father and mother, and shall be joined unto his wife, and they two shall be one flesh. This mystery is great; but I speak of Christ, and of the congregation. Nevertheless, let every one of you so love his own wife, even as himself [Ephes. 5:25-33].

Likewise the same St. Paul, writing to the Colossians, speaketh thus to all men that be married: Ye men, love your wives, and be not bitter unto them [Col. 3:19].

Hear also what St. Peter, the Apostle of Christ, which was himself a married man, saith unto all men that are married: Ye husbands, dwell with your wives according to knowledge; giving honour unto the wife, as unto the weaker vessel, and as heirs together of the grace of life, so that your prayers be not hindered [1 Peter 3:7].

Hitherto ye have heard the duty of the husband toward the wife. Now likewise, ye wives, hear and learn your duties toward your husbands, even as it is plainly set forth in holy Scripture.

St. Paul, in the aforenamed Epistle to the Ephesians, teacheth you thus: Ye women, submit yourselves unto your own husbands, as unto the Lord. For the husband is the wife's head, even as Christ is the head of the Church: and he is also the Saviour of the whole body.

Therefore as the Church of congregation is subject unto Christ, so likewise let the wives also be in subjection to their own husbands in all things [Ephes. 5:22-24]. And again he saith: Let the wife reverence her husband [Ephes. 5:33]. And in his Epistle to the Colossians, St.

Paul giveth you this short lesson: Ye wives, submit yourselves unto your own husbands, as it is convenient in the Lord [Col. 3:18].

St. Peter also doth instruct you very godly, thus saying: Let wives, be subject to their own husbands, so that if any obey not the Word, they may be won without the Word, by the conversation of the wives, while they behold your chaste conversation coupled with fear. Whose apparell, let it not be outward with braided hair, and trimming about with gold, either in putting on of gorgeous apparel. But let the hid man which is in the heart, be without all corruption, so that the spirit be mild and quiet, which is a precious thing in the sight of God. For after this manner in the old time did the holy women, which trusted in God, apparell themselves, being subject to their own husbands: as Sarah obeyed Abraham, calling him lord, whose daughters ye are made doing well, and not being dismayed with any fear [1 Peter 3:1-6].

5. James VI and I, *Basilikon Doron* (first published 1599). Rpt. in *The works of the most high and mighty prince, James by the grace of God, King of Great Britain, France and Ireland, Defender of the Faith*, 1616 (STC 14344), 173.

And for your behaviour to your wife, the Scripture can best give you counsel therein. Treat her as your own flesh, command her as her lord, cherish her as your helper, rule her as your pupil, and please her in all things reasonable. But teach her not to be curious in things that belong her not: ye are the head, she is your body. It is your office to command and hers to obey, but yet with such a sweet harmony, as she should be as ready to obey as ye to command, as willing to follow as ye to go before, your love being wholly knit unto her, and all her affections lovingly bent to follow your will.

And to conclude, keep specially three rules with your wife. First, suffer her never to meddle with the politic government of the commonwealth, but hold her at the economic rule of the house, and yet all to be subject to your direction. Keep carefully good and chaste company about her, for women are the frailest sex. And be never both angry at once, but when ye see her in passion ye should with reason danton yours, for both when ye are settled, ye are meetest to judge of her errors, and when she is come to herself, she may be best made to apprehend her offence, and reverence your rebuke.

6. James VI and I, *The true law of free monarchies* (first published 1603). Rpt. in *The works of the Most High and Mighty Prince, James by the Grace of God, King of Great Britain, France and Ireland, Defender of the Faith*, 1616 (STC 14344), 195; 204.

By the law of nature the King becomes a natural father to all his lieges at his coronation, and the father of his fatherly duty is bound to care for the nourishing, education, and virtuous government of his children. Even so is the King bound to care for all his subjects. As all the toil and pain that the father can take for his children, will be thought light and well bestowed by him, so that the effect thereof redound to their profit and weal: so ought the Prince to do towards his people. As the kindly father ought to foresee all inconvenients and dangers that may arise towards his children and, though with the hazard of his own person, press to prevent the same: so ought the King towards his people. As the father's wrath and correction upon any of his children that offendeth, ought to be by a fatherly chastisement seasoned with pity, as long as there is any hope of amendment in them, so ought the King towards any of his lieges that offends in that measure. And shortly, as the father's chief joy ought to be in procuring his children's welfare, rejoicing at their weal, sorrowing and pitying at their evil, to hazard for their safety, travail for their rest, wake for their sleep, and in a word, to think that his earthly felicity and life standeth and liveth more in them, nor in himself; so ought a good Prince think of his people. . . .

And the agreement of the law of nature in this our ground with the laws and constitutions of God and man, already alleged, will by two similitudes easily appear. The King towards his people is rightly compared to a father of children, and to a head of a body composed of divers members. For as fathers, the good Princes and Magistrates of the people of God acknowledged themselves to their subjects. And for all other well ruled commonwealths, the style of *Pater patriae* was ever, and is commonly used to Kings. And the proper office of a King towards his subjects agrees very well with the office of the head towards the body, and all members thereof. For from the head, being the seat of judgement, proceedeth the care and foresight of guiding and preventing all evil that may come to the body, or any part thereof. The head cares for the body, so doth the King for his people. As the discourse and direction flows from the head, and the execution according thereunto belongs to the rest of the members, every one according to his office, so is it betwixt a wise Prince and his people. As the judgement coming from the head may not only employ the members, every one in their own office, as long as they are able for it; but likewise in case any of them be affected with any infirmity, must care and provide for their remedy, in case it be curable, and if otherwise, cut them off for fear of infecting the rest. Even so is it betwixt the Prince and his people. And as there is ever hope of curing any diseased member by the direction of the head, as long as it is whole, but by the contrary, if it be troubled, all the members are partakers of that pain, so it is betwixt the Prince and his people.

7. Dorothy Leigh, *The Mothers Blessing. Or, the godly counsel of a gentlewoman not long since deceased, left behind her for her children*, 1616 (STC 15402), 29-34; 35-40.

The names I have chosen you are these: Philip, Elizabeth, James, Anna, John and Susanna. The virtues of them that bore those names, and the causes why I chose them, I let pass and only mean to write of the last name. Susan, famoused through the world for chastity, a virtue which always hath been, and is of great account, not only amongst the Christians and people of God, but even among the heathen and infidels, insomuch that some of them have written, that a woman that is truly chaste, is a great partaker of all other virtues, and contrariwise, that the woman that is not truly chaste, hath no virtue in her. The which saying may well be warranted by the Scripture: for who is truly chaste, is free from idleness and from all vain delights, full of humility, and all good Christian virtues. Who so is chaste is not given to pride in apparel, nor any vanity, but is always either reading, meditating, or practising some good thing which she hath learned in the Scripture. But she which is unchaste, is given to be idle. Or if she do anything, it is for a vain glory, and for the praise of men, more than for any humble, loving and obedient heart, that she beareth unto God and his Word, who said: Six days thou shalt labour [Exod. 20:9], and so left no time for idleness, pride, or vanity; for in none of these is there any holiness. The unchaste woman is proud, and always decking herself with vanity, and delights to hear the vain words of men, in which there is not only vanity, but also so much wickedness, that the vain words of men, and women's vainness in hearing them, hath brought many women to much sorrow and vexation; as woeful experience hath, and will, make many of them confess. But some will say, had they only lent an ear to their words they had done well enough. To answer which, I would have every one know, that one sin begetteth another. The vain words of the man, and the idle cares of the woman, beget unchaste thoughts oftentimes in the one, which may bring forth much wickedness in them both.

Man said once: The woman which thou gavest me, beguiled me, and I did eat [Gen. 3:12]. But we women may now say, that men lie in wait everywhere to deceive us, and the Elders did to deceive Susanna. Wherefore let us be, as she was, chaste, watchful, and wary, keeping company with maids. Once Judas betrayed his Master with a kiss, and repented it. But now men like Judas, betray their mistresses with a kiss and, repent it not, but laugh and rejoice, that they have brought sin and shame to her that trusted them. The only way to avoid all which, is to be chaste with Susanna, and being women, to embrace that virtue, which being placed in a woman is most commendable.

An unchaste woman destroyeth both the body and the soul of him she seemeth most to love, and it is almost impossible to set down the mischiefs, which have come through unchaste women. Solomon saith that, her steps lead to hell [Prov. 2.18]. Wherefore, bring up your daughters, as Susanna's parents brought her up:

teach them the law of the Lord continually, and always persuade them to embrace this virtue of chastity. . . .

For before, men might say: The woman beguiled me and I did eat the poisoned fruit of disobedience, and I die. But now man may say, if he say truly: The woman brought me a Saviour, and I feed of him by faith and live. Here is the great and woeful shame taken from women by God, working in a woman; man can claim no part in it. The shame is taken from us, and from out posterity forever: The seed of the woman hath taken down the Serpent's head [Gen. 3:15]; and now whosoever can take hold of the seed of the woman by faith, shall surely live for ever. And therefore all generations shall say that she was blessed, who brought us a Saviour, the fruit of obedience, that whosoever feedeth of, shall live forever, and except they feed of the seed of the woman, they have no life [John 6:53]. Will not therefore all women seek out this great grace of God, that by Mary hath taken away the shame, which before was due unto us ever since the fall of man?

Mary was filled with the Holy Ghost, and with all goodness, and yet is called the blessed Virgin, as if our God should (as he doth indeed) in brief comprehend all other virtues under this one virtue of chastity. Wherefore I desire, that all women, what name soever they bear, would learn of this blessed Virgin to be chaste. For though she were more replenished with grace than any other, and more freely beloved of the Lord, yet the greatest title that she had, was that she was a blessed and pure Virgin, which is a great cause to move all women whether they be maids or wives (both which estates she honoured) to live chastely. To whom for this cause God hath given a cold and temperate disposition, and bound them with these words: Thy desire shall be subject to thy husband [Gen. 3:16]. As if God in mercy to women should say: You of yourselves shall have no desires, only they shall be subject to your husband's. Which hath been verified in heathen women, so as it is almost incredible to be believed, for many of them before they would be defiled, have been careless of their lives, and so have endured all those torments, that men would devise to inflict upon them, rather than they would lose the name of a modest maid, or a chaste matron. Yea, and so far they have been from consenting to any immodesty, that if at any time they have been ravished, they have either made away themselves, or at least have separated themselves from company, not thinking themselves worthy of any society, after they have once been deflowered, though against their wills. Wherefore the woman that is infected with the sin of uncleanness, is worse than a beast, because it desireth but for nature, and she, to satisfy her corrupt lusts.

Some of the Fathers have written that it is not enough for a woman to be chaste, but even so to behave herself that no man may think or deem her to be unchaste.

8. Rachel Speght, *A Muzzle for Melastomus, The Cynical Baiter of, and foul mouthed barker against Evah's sex,* 1617 (STC 23058), 14-18.

Marriage is a merri-age, and this world's Paradise, where there is mutual love. Our blessed Saviour vouchsafed to honour a marriage with the first miracle that he wrought [John 2:1-11], unto which miracle matrimonial estate may not unfitly be resembled. For as Christ turned water into wine, a far more excellent liquor, which, as the Psalmist saith: Makes glad the heart of man [Psal. 104:15], so the single man is by marriage changed from a bachelor to a husband, a far more excellent title, from a solitary life unto a joyful union and conjunction, with such a creature as God hath made meet for man, for whom none was meet till she was made. . . . A virtuous woman, saith Solomon, is the crown of her husband [Prov. 12:4], by which metaphor he showeth both the excellency of such a wife, and what account her husband is to make of her. For a king doth not trample his crown under his feet, but highly esteems of it, gently handles it, and carefully lays it up, as the evidence of his kingdom. And therefore when David destroyed Rabbah he took off the crown from their King's head [1 Chron. 20:2]. So husbands should not account their wives as their vassals, but as those that are herein together of the grace of life, and with all lenity and mild persuasions set their feet in the right way, if they happen to tread awry, bearing with their infirmities, as Elkanah did with his wife's barrenness [1 Samuel 1:8].

The kingdom of God is compared unto the marriage of a king's son: John calleth the conjunction of Christ and his chosen, a marriage [Rev. 19:7]. And not few, but many times, doth our blessed Saviour in the Canticles, set forth his unspeakable love towards his Church under the title of an husband rejoicing with his wife; and often vouchsafeth to call her his sister and spouse, by which is showed that with God is no respect of persons, nations, or sexes [Rom. 2:11]. For whosoever, whether it be man or woman, that doth believe in the Lord Jesus, such shall be saved [John 3:15-18]. And if God's love even from the beginning, had not been as great toward woman as to man, then would he not have preserved from the deluge of the old world as many women as men, nor would Christ after his resurrection have appeared unto a woman first of all other, had it not been to declare thereby, that the benefits of his death and resurrection, are as available, by belief, for women as for men. For he indifferently died for the one sex as well as the other. Yet a truth ungainsayable is it, that the man is the woman's head [1 Cor. 11:3], by which title yet of supremacy, no authority hath he given him to domineer, or basely command and employ his wife, as a servant, but hereby is he taught the duties which he oweth unto her. For as the head of a man is the imaginer and contriver of projects profitable for the safety of his whole body, so the husband must protect and defend his wife from injuries: For he is her head, as Christ is the head of his Church [Ephes. 5:23], which he entirely loveth, and for which he gave his very life; the dearest thing any man hath in this world [Job 2:4]. Greater love than this hath no man, when he bestoweth his life for his friend, saith our Saviour [John 15:13]. This precedent passeth all other patterns, it requireth great benignity, and enjoineth an extraordinary affection, for men must love their wives, even as Christ loved his Church. Secondly, as the head doth not jar or contend with the members, which being many, as the Apostle saith, yet make but one body [1 Cor. 12:20]. No more must the husband with the wife, but expelling all bitterness and cruelty he must live with her lovingly [Col. 3:19], and religiously, honouring her as the weaker vessel [1 Peter 3:7]. Thirdly, and lastly, as he is her head, he must, by instruction, bring her to the knowledge of her Creator [1 Cor. 14:35], that so she may be a fit stone for the Lord's building. Women for this end must have an especial care to set their affections upon such as are able to teach them, that as they grow in years, they may grow in grace, and in the knowledge of Christ Jesus our Lord.

Thus if men would remember the duties they are to perform in being heads, some would not stand a tip-toe as they do, thinking themselves lords and rulers, and account every omission of performing whatsoever they command, whether lawful or not, to be matter of great disparagement and indignity done them. Whereas they should consider, that women are enjoined to submit themselves unto their husbands no otherwise than as to the Lord [Eph. 5:22]; so that from hence, for man, ariseth a lesson not to be forgotten, that as the Lord commandeth nothing to be done, but that which is right and good, no more must the husband. For if a wife fulfill the evil command of her husband, she obeys him as a tempter, as Saphira did Ananias [Acts 5:2]. But lest I should seem too partial in praising women so much as I have (though no more than warrant from Scripture doth allow) I add to the premises, that I say not, all women are virtuous, for then they should be more excellent than men, sith of Adam's sons there was Cain as well as Abel, and of Noah's, Cham as well as Sem. So that of men as of women, there are two sorts, namely, good and bad, which in Matthew the five and twenty chapter, are comprehended under the name of Sheep and Goats [Math. 25:31-33].

9. Ester Sowernam, *Ester Hath Hang'd Haman: Or, an Answer to a lewd Pamphlet, entitled, the Arraignment of Women. With the arraignment of lewd, idle, froward and unconstant men, and husbands,* 1617 (STC 22974), 5-6.
From Chapter II, "What incomparable and excellent prerogatives God hath bestowed upon Women in their first Creation."

It appeareth by that Sovereignty which God gave to Adam over all the creatures of sea and land that man was the end of God's creation, whereupon it doth necessarily without all exception follow, that

Adam, being the last work, is therefore the most excellent work of creation. Yet Adam was not so absolutely perfect, but that in the sight of God, he wanted an helper. Whereupon God created the woman his last work, as to supply and make absolute that imperfect building which was unperfected in man, as all divines do hold, till the happy creation of the woman. Now of what estimate that creature is and ought to be, which is the last work, upon whom the Almighty set up his last rest, whom he made to add perfection to the end of all creation, I leave rather to be acknowledged by others than resolved by myself.

It is furthermore to be considered, as the Maid in her *Muzzle for Melastomus* hath observed, that God intended to honour woman in a more excellent degree, in that he created her out of a subject refined, as out of a quintessence. For the rib is in substance more solid, in place as most near, so in estimate most dear, to man's heart, which doth presage that as she was made for an helper, so to be an helper to stay, to settle all joy, all contents, all delights, to and in man's heart[.]

10. William Whately, *A Bride-Bush*, or *A Wedding Sermon: compendiously describing the duties of married persons*, 1617 (STC 25296), 37; 38-39; 42-43.

29. And first for reverence, the wife owes as much of that to her husband, as the children or servants do to her, yea, as they do to him; only it is allowed that it be sweetened with more love and more familiarity. The wife should not think so erroneously of her place, as if she were not bound equally with the children and servants to reverence her husband: all inferiors owe reverence alike. The difference is only this, she may be more familiar, not more rude than they, as being more dear, not less subject to him....

31. And as the heart principally, so next the outward behaviour must be regarded in three special things. First, in speeches and gestures unto him. These must carry the stamp of fear upon them, and not be cutted, sharp, sullen, passionate, tetchy, but meek, quiet, submissive,

which may show that she considers who herself is, and to whom she speaks. The wife's tongue towards her husband must be neither keen, nor loose, her countenance neither swelling nor deriding, her behaviour not flinging, not puffing, not discontented, but favouring of all lowliness and quietness of affection. Look what kind of words or behaviour thou wouldst dislike from thy servant or child, those must thou not give to thine husband, for thou art equally commanded to be subject.... [W]e have some women that can chafe and scold with their husbands, and rail upon them, and revile them, and shake them together with such terms and carriage, as were unsufferable towards a servant. Stains of woman-kind, blemishes of their sex, monsters in natures, botches of human society, rude, graceless, impudent, next to harlots, if not the same with them. Let such words leave a blister behind them, and let the canker eat out these tongues. But besides these so notorious ones, even women otherwise virtuous, must see their faults in this behalf. They can take up their husbands with quick speeches sharply set on. They can set them down short, with a cutted answer, with a frowning countenance, with a disdainful look, and the side turned towards them in displeasure. Why, wilt thou teach thy children to be rebellious, and show thy servants how to swell, pout, and fume? Thinkest thou such behaviour will not infect? Shall not they also use it to thee? Or is it less tolerable in thee? Be submissive rather, and let them learn reverence from thee to practice to thee. The woman makes herself vile that sets her husband at nought, or else seems to do it....

34. Obedience follows. As concerning which duty a plain text avers it to the full, saying: Let the wife be subject to her husband in all things, in the Lord [Ephes. 5:22]. What need we further proof? Why is she his wife, if she will not obey? And how can she require obedience of the children and servants, if she will not yield to the husband? Doth not she exact it in his name, and as his deputy? But the thing will not be so much questioned, as the measure: not whether she must obey, but how far. Wherefore we must extend it as far as the Apostle, to a generality of things, to all things, so it be

in the Lord. In whatsoever thing obeying of him doth not disobey God, she must obey: and if not in all things, it were as good in nothing. It is a thankless service if not general. To yield alone in things that please herself, is not to obey him, but her own affections. The trial of obedience is when it crosseth her desires. To do that which he bids, when she would have done without his bidding, what praise is it? But this declares conscionable submission, when she chooseth to do what herself would not, because her husband wills it. And seeing she requireth the like largeness of duty in his name from the servants, herself shall be judge against herself, if she give not what she looks to receive. But it sufficeth not that her obedience reach to all things that are lawful, unless it be also willing, ready, without brawling, contending, thwarting, sourness. A good work may be marred in the manner of doing. And as good stuff is spilt by bad making, so doth the wife disgrace and disfigure her obedience if she hang off and contend, and be impatient, and will not, till she cannot choose. Needs must, needs, shall, we say in the proverb. Such kind of yielding declares no reverence, deserves no praise. Then it is laudable, commendable, a note of a virtuous woman, a dutiful wife, when she submits herself with quietness, cheerfully, even as a well-broken horse turns at the least turning, stands at the least check of the rider's bridle, readily going and standing as he wishes that sits upon his back. If you will have your obedience worth anything, make no tumult about it outwardly, allow none within.

11. Elizabeth Jocelin, *The Mother's Legacy to her Unborn Child*, 1624 (STC 14624), sigs. B^r-B11^v.
From "Epistle Dedicatory, To My Truly Loving and Most Dearly Loved Husband, Turrell Jocelin."

Mine own dear love, I no sooner conceived an hope, that I should be made a mother by thee, but with it entered the consideration of a mother's duty, and shortly after followed the apprehension of danger that might prevent me from executing that care I so exceedingly desired. I mean in religious training our child. And in truth, death appearing in this shape, was doubly terrible unto me. First, in respect of the painfulness of that kind of death, and next of the loss my little one should have in wanting me.

But I thank God, these fears were cured with the remembrance that all things work together for the best to those that love God, and a certain assurance that he will give me patience according to my pain.

Yet still I thought there was some good office I might do for my child, more than only to bring it forth (though it should please God to take me). When I considered our frailty, our apt inclination to sin, the devil's subtlety, and the world's deceitfulness against these, how much desired I to admonish it? But still it came into my mind that death might deprive me of time if I should neglect the present. I knew not what to do. I thought of writing, but then mine own weakness appeared so manifestly, that I was ashamed, and durst not undertake it. But when I could find no other means to express my motherly zeal, I encouraged myself with these reasons.

First, that I wrote to a child, and though I were but a woman, yet to a child's judgement, what I understood might serve for a foundation to better learning.

Again, I considered it was to my own, and in private sort, and my love to my own might excuse my errors.

And lastly, but chiefly, I comforted myself, that my intent was good, and that I was well assured God is the prosperer of good purposes....

[I]f it be a son, I doubt not but thou wilt dedicate it to the Lord as his minister, if he will please of his mercy to give him grace and capacity for that great work. If it be a daughter, I hope my mother Brook (if thou desirest her) will take it among hers, and let them all learn one lesson.

I desire her bringing up may be learning the Bible, as my sisters do, good housewifery, writing, and good works. Other learning a woman needs not, though I admire it in those whom God hath blessed with discretion, yet I desire it not much in my own, having seen that sometimes women have greater portions of learning, than wisdom, which is of no better use to them than a main-sail to a fly-boat, which runs it under water. But where learning and wisdom meet in a virtuous disposed woman, she is the fittest closet for all goodness. She is like a well-balanced ship that may bear all her sail. She is – indeed I should but shame myself, if I should go about to praise her more.

But, my dear, though she have all this in her, she will hardly make a poor man's wife. Yet I leave it to thy will. If thou desirest a learned daughter, I pray God give her a wise and religious heart, that she may use it to his glory, thy comfort, and her own salvation.

But howsoever thou disposest of her education, I pray thee labour by all means to teach her true humility, though I much desire it may be as humble if it be a son as a daughter. Yet in a daughter I more fear that vice, pride, being now rather accounted a virtue in our sex worthy praise, than a vice fit for reproof.

Many parents read lectures of it to their children how necessary it is, and they have principles that must not be disputed against. As first, look how much you esteem yourself, others will esteem of you. Again, what you give to others, you derogate from yourself. And many more of these kinds. I have heard men accounted wise that have maintained this kind of pride under the name of generous knowing or understanding themselves. But I am sure that he that truly knows himself shall know so much evil by himself, that he shall have small reason to think himself better than another man.

Dearest, I am so fearful to bring thee a proud, high minded child, that, though I know thy care will need no spur, yet I cannot but desire thee to double thy watchfulness over this vice. It is such a crafty, insinuating devil, it will enter little children in the likeness of wit, with which their parents are delighted, and that is sweet nourishment to it.

I pray thee, dear heart, delight not to have a bold child; modesty and humility are the sweetest groundworks for all virtue. Let not thy servants give it any other title than the Christian-name, till it have discretion to understand how to respect others.

Appendix C: Photographs from the Tinderbox Theatre Company Production of The Tragedy of Mariam *[Photography by Stuart Ellis]*

Sohemus (Andrew Maher) and Mariam (Jo Dyer) in Act III, scene iii.

Mariam (Jo Dyer), Butler (Lou Ford), and Herod (Dave Newport)
in Act IV, scene iv.

Constabarus (Anthony Bentley) and Baba's sons
(Andrew Maher, Graeme Watson) in Act IV, scene vi.

Salome (Suzannah Rogers) and Herod (Dave Newport) in
Act IV, scene vii.

Bibliography

Works Cited

Beilin, Elaine. *Redeeming Eve: Women Writers of the English Renaissance*. Guildford: Princeton University Press, 1987.

Belsey, Catherine. *The Subject of Tragedy: Identity and Difference in Renaissance Drama*. London: Methuen, 1985.

Callaghan, Dympna. "Re-Reading Elizabeth Cary's *The Tragedie of Mariam, Faire Queene of Jewry*." *Women, "Race," and Writing in the Early Modern Period*. Ed. Margo Hendricks and Patricia Parker. London: Routledge, 1994. 163-77.

Cary ? Biography of Lady Falkland, c. 1650, MS A.D.N.xx., Archives dèpartementales du Nord, Lille.

Cerasano, S.P., and Marion Wynne-Davies, eds. *The Tragedy of Mariam*. In their *Renaissance Drama by Women*. London: Routledge, 1995.

Cotton, Nancy. *Women Playwrights in England, 1363-1750*. London: Associated University Presses, 1980.

Davies, John. *The Muses Sacrifice*. London: 1612, STC 6338.

Drayton, Michael. *Englands Heroicall Epistles*. London: 1597, STC 7193.

Dunstan, A.C., ed. *The Tragedy of Mariam* (1914). Rpt. with a supplement by Marta Straznicky and Richard Rowland. Oxford: Malone Society, 1992.

Ferguson, Margaret. "The Spectre of Resistance." *Staging the Renaissance: Reinterpretations of Elizabethan and Jacobean Drama*. Ed. David Scott Kastan and Peter Stallybrass. London: Routledge, 1992. 233-50.

—. "Renaissance Concepts of the 'Woman Writer.'" *Women and Literature in Britain 1500-1700*. Ed. Helen Wilcox. Cambridge: Cambridge University Press, 1996. 143-68.

Findlay, Alison, Stephanie Hodgson-Wright, and Gweno Williams. "'The Play is Ready to be Acted': Women and Dramatic Production 1550-1670." *Women's Writing: The*

Elizabethan to Victorian Period 6:1 (1999):129-48.

—. "Performing Early Modern Drama by Women." *Attending to Early Modern Women 1997.* Ed. Jane Donawerth and Adele Seef. Newark: University of Delaware Press (forthcoming).

Fischer, Sandra K. "Elizabeth Cary and Tyranny, Religious and Domestic." *Silent but for the Word: Tudor Women as Patrons, Translators and Writers of Religious Works.* Ed. Margaret P. Hannay. Ohio: Kent State University Press, 1985. 225-37.

Gutierrez, Nancy. "Valuing *Mariam*: Genre Study and Feminist Analysis." *Tulsa Studies in Women's Literature* 10:2 (1991): 233-51.

Hackett, Helen, "Courtly Writing by Women." *Women and Literature in Britain 1500-1700.* Ed. Helen Wilcox. Cambridge: Cambridge University Press, 1996. 169-89.

Hannay, Margaret P. *Philip's Phoenix: Mary Sidney, Countess of Pembroke.* Oxford: Oxford University Press, 1990.

Hardy, Alexandre. *Mariamne* (1605?). Ed. and trans. Lacy Lockert. In *More Plays by Rivals of Corneille and Racine.* Nashville: Vanderbilt University Press, 1968.

Holdsworth, R.V. "Middleton and *The Tragedy of Mariam*." *Notes & Queries* 231 (1986): 379-80.

Irigaray, Luce. "Ce sexe qui n'en est pas un" (This sex which is not one). In *Ce sexe qui n'en est pas un.* Minuit: 1977. Trans. Claudia Reeder. Rpt. in *New French Feminisms.* Ed. Elaine Marks and Isabelle de Courtivron. Brighton: Harvester, 1981. 99-106.

Josephus, Flavius. *The most auncient historie of the Jewes: comprised in twenty books.* Trans. Thomas Lodge. London: 1602, STC 14809.

Kemp, Theresa. "The Family is a Little Commonwealth: Teaching *Mariam* and *Othello* in a Special-Topics Course on Domestic England." *Shakespeare Quarterly* 47:4 (1996): 451-60.

Kennedy, Gwynne. "Lessons of the 'Schoole of Wisedom.'" *Sexuality and Politics in Renaissance Drama.* Ed. Carole Levin and Karen Robertson. Lampeter: The Edwin Mellen Press, 1991. 113-36.

Krontiris, Tina. *Oppositional Voices: Women as Writers and Translators of Literature in the English Renaissance.* London: Routledge, 1992.

Levin, Richard. "A Possible Source for *A Fair Quarrel.*" *Notes & Queries 228* (1983): 152-53.

Lewalski, Barbara Keifer. *Writing Women in Jacobean England.* London: Harvard University Press, 1993.

Lindley, David, ed. *The Court Masque.* Oxford: Oxford University Press, 1995.

McClure, N.E., ed. *The Letters of John Chamberlain.* Vol. I. Philadelphia: The American Philosphical Society, 1939.

Markham, Gervase, and William Sampson. *The True Tragedy of Herod and Antipater: With the Death of Faire Mariam. According to Josephus, that learned and famous Jew,* London: 1622, STC 17401.

—. *The True Tragedy of Herod and Antipater* (1622). Ed. Gordon Nicholas Ross, London: Garland Publishing, 1979.

Newdigate, Bernard. *Michael Drayton and his Circle.* Oxford: Basil Blackwell, 1941.

Raber, Karen L. "Gender and the Political Subject in *The Tragedy of Mariam.*" *Studies in English Literature 1500-1900* 35:2 (1995): 321-41.

Shannon, Laurie J. "*The Tragedie of Mariam*: Cary's Critique of the Terms of Founding Social Discourses." *English Literary Renaissance* 24 (1994): 135-53.

Simpson, Richard, ed. *The Lady Falkland, Her Life.* London: Catholic Publishing and Bookselling Co, 1861.

Skura, Meredith. "The Reproduction of Mothering in *Mariam Queen of Jewry*: A Defense of Biographical Criticism." *Tulsa Studies in Women's Literature* 16:1 (1997): 27-56.

Straznicky, Marta. "'Profane Stoical Paradoxes': *The Tragedie of Mariam* and Sidnean Closet Drama." *English Literary Renaissance* 24 (1994): 104-34.

Travitsky, Betty, ed. *The Paradise of Women: Writings by English-women of the Renaissance.* London: Greenwood Press, 1981.

Weller, Barry, and Margaret Ferguson, eds. *The Tragedy of*

Mariam with The Lady Falkland: Her Life. London: University of California Press, 1994.

Further Reading

Works and editions of works by and attributed to Elizabeth Cary

Cary (neé Tanfield), Elizabeth, "The Mirror of the Worlde translated Out of French into Englishe," by E.T., c. 1598. Bodleian Library, Dep. d. 187.

The Tragedy of Mariam. London: 1613, STC 4613.

The Tragedy of Mariam, ed. A.C. Dunstan. London: Malone Society, 1914.

The Tragedy of Mariam, ed. A.C. Dunstan. Rpt. with a supplement by Marta Straznicky and Richard Rowland. Oxford: Malone Society, 1992.

The Tragedy of Mariam. In *Renaissance Women: The Poems of Aemilia Lanyer and the Plays of Elizabeth Cary.* Ed. Diane Purkiss. London: Pickering and Chatto, 1994.

The Tragedy of Mariam. In *Renaissance Drama by Women.* Ed. S.P. Cerasano and Marion Wynne-Davies. London: Routledge, 1995.

The Tragedy of Mariam. In *Major Women Writers of Seventeenth-Century England.* Ed. James Fitzmaurice, Josephine A. Roberts, Carol L. Barash, Eugene R. Cunnar, and Nancy A. Gutierrez. Ann Arbor: University of Michigan Press, 1997.

The Tragedy of Mariam. In *Three Tragedies by Renaissance Women.* Ed. Diane Purkiss. London: Penguin, 1998.

(Attrib.) "Edwarde the Second: His Raigne, and death with the ffall of those too his greate favorites Gavestone and Spencer," c. 1626. Northamptonshire Record Office, MS Finch-Hatton 1.

(Attrib.) *The History of the Life, Reign and Death of Edward II,* written by E.F. in the year 1627. London: 1680, Wing F313.

(Attrib.) *The Parallel: or the History of the Life, Reign, Deposition and*

Death of Edward the Second, with an Account of His Favourites, P. Gaveston and the Spencers. London: 1689, Wing F314a.

(Attrib.) The History of the Life, Reign and Death of Edward II. In Renaissance Women: The Poems of Aemilia Lanyer and the Plays of Elizabeth Cary. Ed. Diane Purkiss. London: Pickering and Chatto, 1994.

(Attrib.) "An Epitaph upon the death of the Duke of Buckingham by the Countesse of Faukland." British Library, MS Egerton 2725, fol. 60.

Davy, Jacques, Cardinal du Perron. The Reply of the Most Illustrious Cardinall of Perron. Trans. Elizabeth Cary. Douay: 1630, STC 6385.

Davy, Jacques, Cardinal du Perron. The Reply of the Most Illustrious Cardinall of Perron. Trans. Elizabeth Cary, ed. D.M. Rogers. Ilkley: The Scholar Press, 1975.

Anthologies reproducing selections from Cary's writings

Greer, Germaine, Susan Hastings, Jeslyn Medoff, and Melinda Sansome, eds. Kissing the Rod: An Anthology of Seventeenth Century Women's Verse. London: Virago, 1988.

Mahl, Mary R., and Helene Koon, eds. The Female Spectator: English Women Writers Before 1800. London: Indiana University Press, 1977.

Martin, Randall, ed. Women Writers in Renaissance England. London: Longman, 1997.

Travitsky, Betty, ed. The Paradise of Women: Writings by Englishwomen of the Renaissance. London: Greenwood Press, 1981.

Critical and Biographical Works

Beilin, Elaine. "Elizabeth Cary and The Tragedie of Mariam." Papers on Language and Literature 16 (1980): 45-64.

Cary ? *The Lady Falkland, Her Life.* Ed. Richard Simpson.
London: Catholic Publishing and Bookselling Co., 1861.

Cary ? *The Lady Falkland, Her Life.* Ed. Barry Weller and Margaret
W. Ferguson. London: University of California Press, 1994.

Cotton, Nancy. "Elizabeth Cary, Renaissance Playwright." *Texas
Studies in Language and Literature* 18 (1977): 601-08.

The Devon Carys. 2 vols. New York: The Devine Press, 1920.

Fullerton, Lady Georgiana. *The Life of Elisabeth, Lady Falkland.*
London: Burns and Oates, 1883.

Goreau, Angeline. *The Whole Duty of a Woman: Female Writers in
Seventeenth Century England.* New York: Doubleday, 1985.

—. "Two English Women in the Seventeenth Century: Notes for
an Anatomy of Feminine Desire." *Western Sexuality:
Practice and Precept in Past and Present Times.* Ed. Philippe
Ariès and André Béjin, trans. Anthony Foster, Oxford.
Oxford University Press, 1985. 103-13.

Hodgson-Wright, Stephanie. "The Canonization of Elizabeth
Cary." *Voicing Women: Gender and Sexuality in Early
Modern Writing.* Ed. Kate Chegdzoy, Melanie Hansen, and
Susanne Trill. Keele: Keele University Press, 1996. 55-68;
rpt. Edinburgh: Edinburgh University Press, 1998.

Krontiris, Tina. "Reading with the Author's Sex: A Comparison of
Two Seventeenth Century Texts." *Gramma* 1 (1993): 123-36.

Langueville, T. *Falklands.* London: Longmans, Green, and Co., 1897.

Miller, Naomi J. "Domestic Politics in Elizabeth Cary's *The
Tragedy of Mariam.*" *Studies in English Literature 1500-
1900* 37:2 (1997): 353-69.

Murdock, K.B. *Sun at Noon: Three Biographical Sketches.*
New York: Macmillan. 1939.

Nichols, John Gough, ed. *Herald and Genealogist.* Vol. 3.
London: Society of Antiquaries, 1866.

Quilligan, Maureen. "Staging Gender: William Shakespeare and
Elizabeth Cary." *Sexuality and Gender in Early Modern
Europe: Institutions, Texts, Images.* Ed. James Grantham
Turner. Cambridge: Cambridge University Press, 1993.
208-32.

Travitsky, Betty. "The feme covert in Elizabeth Cary's *Mariam*."
  *Ambiguous Realities: Women in the Middle Ages and the
  Renaissance*. Ed. Carole Levin and Jeanie Watson. Detroit:
  Wayne State University Press, 1987. 184-96.
—. "Husband-Murder and Petty Treason in English Renaissance
  Tragedy." *Renaissance Drama* 21 (1991): 171-98.
Valency, Maurice J. *Tragedies of Herod and Mariamme*. New York
  Columbia University Press, 1940.